ITALIAN COOKBOOK 2022

AUTHENTIC FAMILY AND REGIONAL RECIPES

OF THE ITALIAN TRADITION

GIANNI MASTELLA

BENVENUTI

AMICI!!!

TABLE OF CONTENTS

Grilled Marinated Pork Chops 10

Spareribs, Friuli Style 12

Spareribs with Tomato Sauce 14

Spiced Ribs, Tuscan Style 16

Spareribs and Beans 18

Spicy Pork Chops with Pickled Peppers 20

Pork Chops with Rosemary and Apples 22

Pork Chops with Mushroom-Tomato Sauce 24

Pork Chops with Porcini and Red Wine 26

Pork Chops with Cabbage 28

Pork Chops with Fennel and White Wine 30

Pork Chops, Pizzamaker's Style 32

Pork Chops, Molise Style 34

Balsamic-Glazed Pork Tenderloin with Arugula and Parmigiano 36

Herbed Pork Tenderloin 39

Calabrian-Style Pork Tenderloin with Honey and Chile 41

Roast Pork with Potatoes and Rosemary 44

Pork Loin with Lemon 46

Pork Loin with Apples and Grappa 48

Roast Pork with Hazelnuts and Cream 50

Tuscan Pork Loin ... 52

Roast Pork Shoulder with Fennel ... 54

Roast Suckling Pig ... 56

Boneless Spiced Pork Loin Roast ... 59

Braised Pork Shoulder in Milk ... 61

Braised Pork Shoulder with Grapes ... 63

Beer-Braised Pork Shoulder ... 65

Lamb Chops with White Wine ... 67

Lamb Chops with Capers, Lemon, and Sage ... 69

Lamb Chops in Crispy Coating ... 71

Lamb Chops with Artichokes and Olives ... 73

Lamb Chops with Tomato, Caper, and Anchovy Sauce ... 75

"Burn-the-Fingers" Lamb Chops ... 77

Grilled Lamb, Basilicata Style ... 79

Grilled Lamb Skewers ... 81

Lamb Stew with Rosemary, Mint, and White Wine ... 83

Umbrian Lamb Stew with Chickpea Puree ... 85

Hunter's-Style Lamb ... 88

Lamb, Potato, and Tomato Stew ... 91

Lamb and Pepper Stew ... 93

Lamb Casserole with Eggs ... 95

Lamb or Kid with Potatoes, Sicilian Style ... 98

Apulian Lamb and Potato Casserole 101

Lamb Shanks with Chickpeas 104

Lamb Shanks with Peppers and Prosciutto 106

Lamb Shanks with Capers and Olives 109

Lamb Shanks in Tomato Sauce 111

Lamb Pot Roast with Cloves, Roman Style 113

Oranges in Orange Syrup 116

Oranges Gratinéed with Zabaglione 118

White Peaches in Asti Spumante 120

Peaches in Red Wine 121

Amaretti-Stuffed Peaches 122

Pears in Orange Sauce 124

Pears with Marsala and Cream 126

Pears with Warm Chocolate Sauce 128

Rum-Spiced Pears 130

Spiced Pears with Pecorino 132

Roasted Brussels Sprouts 134

Brussels Sprouts with Pancetta 136

Browned Cabbage with Garlic 138

Shredded Cabbage with Capers and Olives 140

Cabbage with Smoked Pancetta 142

Fried Cardoons 143

Cardoons with Parmigiano-Reggiano 145

Cardoons in Cream 146

Carrots and Turnips with Marsala 148

Roasted Carrots with Garlic and Olives 150

Carrots in Cream 151

Sweet-and-Sour Carrots 153

Marinated Eggplant with Garlic and Mint 155

Grilled Eggplant with Fresh Tomato Salsa 157

Eggplant and Mozzarella "Sandwiches" 159

Eggplant with Garlic and Herbs 161

Neapolitan-Style Eggplant Sticks with Tomatoes 163

Eggplant Stuffed with Prosciutto and Cheese 165

Eggplant Stuffed with Anchovies, Capers, and Olives 168

Eggplant with Vinegar and Herbs 171

Fried Eggplant Cutlets 173

Eggplant with Spicy Tomato Sauce 175

Eggplant Parmigiana 177

Roasted Fennel 179

Fennel with Parmesan Cheese 181

Fennel with Anchovy Sauce 183

Green Beans with Parsley and Garlic 185

Green Beans with Hazelnuts 187

Green Beans with Green Sauce ... 189

Green Bean Salad ... 190

Green Beans in Tomato-Basil Sauce ... 192

Green Beans with Pancetta and Onion ... 194

Green Beans with Tomato and Pancetta Sauce ... 196

Green Beans with Parmigiano ... 198

Wax Beans with Olives ... 200

Spinach with Lemon ... 202

Spinach or Other Greens with Butter and Garlic ... 204

Spinach with Raisins and Pine Nuts ... 206

Spinach with Anchovies, Piedmont Style ... 208

Escarole with Garlic ... 210

Dandelion with Potatoes ... 212

Mushrooms with Garlic and Parsley ... 214

Mushrooms, Genoa Style ... 216

Roasted Mushrooms ... 218

Grilled Marinated Pork Chops

Braciole di Maiale ai Ferri

Makes 6 servings

This is a great recipe for quick summer dinners. To test pork chops for doneness, make a small cut near the bone. The meat should still be slightly pink.

1 cup dry white wine

¼ cup olive oil

1 small onion, thinly sliced

1 garlic clove, finely chopped

1 tablespoon chopped fresh rosemary

1 tablespoon chopped fresh sage

6 center-cut pork loin chops, about ¾ inch thick

Lemon wedges, for garnish

1. Combine the wine, oil, onion, garlic, and herbs in a baking dish large enough to hold the chops in a single layer. Add the chops, cover, and refrigerate for at least 1 hour.

2. Place a barbecue grill or broiler rack about 5 inches from the heat source. Preheat the grill or broiler. Pat the chops dry with paper towels.

3. Grill the meat 5 to 8 minutes, or until nicely browned. Turn the chops over with tongs and cook on the other side for 6 minutes, or until browned and just slightly pink when cut near the bone. Serve hot, garnished with lemon wedges.

Spareribs, Friuli Style

Spuntature di Maiale alla Friulana

Makes 4 to 6 servings

In Fruili, spareribs are simmered slowly until the meat is tender and falling away from the bone. Serve them with mashed potatoes or a plain risotto.

2 cups homemade Meat Broth or store-bought beef broth

3 pounds pork spareribs, cut into individual ribs

¾ cup all-purpose flour

Salt and freshly ground black pepper

3 tablespoons olive oil

1 large onion, chopped

2 medium carrots, chopped

½ cup dry white wine

1. Prepare the broth, if necessary. Pat the ribs dry with paper towels.

2. On a piece of wax paper, combine the flour and salt and pepper to taste. Roll the ribs in the flour, then shake them to remove the excess.

3. In a wide heavy saucepan, heat the oil over medium heat. Add as many ribs as will fit comfortably in a single layer and brown them well on all sides, about 15 minutes. Transfer the ribs to a plate. Repeat until all of the ribs are browned. Drain off all but 2 tablespoons of the fat.

4. Add the onion and carrots to the pan. Cook, stirring occasionally, until lightly browned, about 10 minutes. Add the wine and cook 1 minute, scraping up and blending in the browned bits at the bottom of the pan with a wooden spoon. Return the ribs to the pan and add the broth. Bring the liquid to a simmer. Reduce the heat to low, cover, and cook, stirring occasionally, about $1^{1}/_{2}$ hours, or until the meat is very tender and coming away from the bones. (Add water if the meat becomes too dry.)

5. Transfer the ribs to a warm serving platter and serve immediately.

Spareribs with Tomato Sauce

Spuntature al Pomodoro

Makes 4 to 6 servings

My husband and I had spareribs like these at a favorite osteria, a casual family-style restaurant in Rome called Enoteca Corsi. It is only open for lunch, and the menu is very limited. But every day it is packed with hordes of workers from nearby offices attracted by its very fair prices and delicious homestyle food.

2 tablespoons olive oil

3 pounds pork spareribs, cut into individual ribs

Salt and freshly ground black pepper

1 medium onion, finely chopped

1 medium carrot, finely chopped

1 tender celery rib, finely chopped

2 garlic cloves, finely chopped

4 sage leaves, chopped

½ cup dry white wine

2 cups canned crushed tomatoes

1. In a Dutch oven or wide, heavy saucepan, heat the oil over medium heat. Add just enough of the ribs to fit comfortably in the pan. Brown them well on all sides, about 15 minutes. Transfer the ribs to a plate. Sprinkle with salt and pepper. Continue with the remaining ribs. When all are done, spoon off all but 2 tablespoons of the fat.

2. Add the onion, carrot, celery, garlic, and sage, and cook until wilted, about 5 minutes. Stir in the wine and bring to a simmer 1 minute, stirring with a wooden spoon and scraping up and blending in the browned bits at the bottom of the pan.

3. Return the ribs to the pan. Add the tomatoes, and salt and pepper to taste. Cook 1 to 1½ hours, or until the ribs are very tender and the meat is coming away from the bones.

4. Transfer ribs and tomato sauce to a serving plate and serve immediately.

Spiced Ribs, Tuscan Style

Spuntature alla Toscana

Makes 4 to 6 servings

With friends from the Lucini olive oil company, I visited the home of olive growers in the Chianti region of Tuscany. Our group of journalists ate lunch in a grove of olive trees. After various bruschette and salami, we were served steak, sausages, ribs, and vegetables, all grilled over grapevine cuttings. The pork ribs marinated in a tasty rub of olive oil and crushed spices were my favorite, and we all tried to guess what was in the mix. Cinnamon and fennel were easy, but we were all surprised to learn another spice was star anise. I like to use little baby-back ribs for this recipe, but spareribs would be fine, too.

2 star anise

1 tablespoon fennel seeds

6 juniper berries, lightly crushed with the side of a heavy knife

1 tablespoon kosher or fine sea salt

1 teaspoon cinnamon

1 teaspoon finely ground black pepper

Pinch of crushed red pepper

4 tablespoons olive oil

4 pounds baby-back ribs, cut into individual ribs

1. In a spice grinder or blender, combine the star anise, fennel, juniper, and salt. Grind until fine, about 1 minute.

2. In a large shallow bowl, combine the contents of the spice grinder with the cinnamon and black and red pepper. Add the oil and stir well. Rub the mixture all over the ribs. Place the ribs in the bowl. Cover with plastic wrap and refrigerate 24 hours, stirring occasionally.

3. Place a barbecue grill or broiler rack about 6 inches from the heat source. Preheat the grill or broiler. Pat the ribs dry, then grill or broil the ribs, turning them frequently, until browned and cooked through, about 20 minutes. Serve hot.

Spareribs and Beans

Puntini e Fagioli

Makes 6 servings

When I know I have a busy week ahead, I like to make up stews like this one. They only improve when made in advance, and need just a quick reheating to make a satisfying dinner. Serve these with cooked greens like spinach or escarole, or a green salad.

2 tablespoons olive oil

3 pounds country-style pork spareribs, cut into individual ribs

1 onion, chopped

1 carrot, chopped

1 garlic clove, finely chopped

2½ pounds fresh tomatoes, peeled, seeded, and chopped, or 1 (28-ounce) can peeled tomatoes, chopped

1 (3-inch) sprig rosemary

1 cup water

Salt and freshly ground black pepper

3 cups cooked or canned cannellini or cranberry beans, drained

1. In a large Dutch oven or other deep, heavy pot with a tight-fitting lid, heat the oil over medium heat. Add just enough of the ribs to fit comfortably in the pan. Brown them well on all sides, about 15 minutes. Transfer the ribs to a plate. Sprinkle with salt and pepper. Continue with the remaining ribs. When all are done, pour off all but 2 tablespoons of the fat.

2. Add the onion, carrot, and garlic to the pot. Cook, stirring frequently, until the vegetables are tender, about 10 minutes. Add the ribs, then the tomatoes, rosemary, water, and salt and pepper to taste. Bring to a simmer over low heat and cook 1 hour.

3. Add the beans, cover, and cook 30 minutes or until the meat is very tender and coming away from the bone. Taste and adjust seasoning. Serve hot.

Spicy Pork Chops with Pickled Peppers

Braciole di Maiale con Peperoncini

Makes 4 servings

Pickled hot chiles and sweet pickled peppers are a fine topping for juicy pork chops. Adjust the proportions of the chiles and sweet peppers to suit your taste. Serve these with fried potatoes.

2 tablespoons olive oil

4 center-cut pork loin chops, each about 1 inch thick

Salt and freshly ground black pepper

4 garlic cloves, thinly sliced

1½ cups sliced pickled sweet peppers

¼ cup sliced pickled hot peppers, such as peperoncini or jalapeños, or more of the sweet peppers

2 tablespoons pickling juice or white wine vinegar

2 tablespoons chopped fresh flat-leaf parsley

1. In a large heavy skillet, heat the oil over medium-high heat. Pat the chops dry with paper towels then sprinkle them with salt and pepper. Cook the chops until browned, about 2 minutes, then turn them over with tongs and brown on the other side, about 2 minutes more.

2. Reduce the heat to medium. Scatter the garlic slices around the chops. Cover the pan and cook 5 to 8 minutes or until the chops are tender and just slightly pink when cut near the bone. Regulate the heat so that the garlic does not become dark brown. Transfer the chops to a serving platter and cover to keep warm.

3. Add the sweet and hot peppers and pickling juice or vinegar to the skillet. Cook, stirring, for 2 minutes or until the peppers are heated through and the juices are syrupy.

4. Stir in the parsley. Spoon the contents of the pan over the chops and serve immediately.

Pork Chops with Rosemary and Apples

Braciole al Mele

Makes 4 servings

The sweet-tart flavor of apples is a perfect complement to pork chops. This recipe is from Friuli– Venezia Giulia.

4 center-cut pork chops, each about 1 inch thick

Salt and freshly ground black pepper

1 tablespoon chopped fresh rosemary

1 tablespoon unsalted butter

4 golden delicious apples, peeled and cut into ½-inch pieces

$1/2$ cup Chicken Broth

1. Pat the meat dry with paper towels. Sprinkle the chops on both sides with the salt, pepper, and rosemary.

2. In a large heavy skillet, melt the butter over medium heat. Add the chops and cook until they are nicely browned on one side, about 2 minutes. Turn the chops over with tongs and brown on the other side, about 2 minutes more.

3. Scatter the apples around the chops and pour in the broth. Cover the skillet and turn the heat to low. Cook about 5 to 10 minutes, turning the chops once, until they are tender and just slightly pink when cut near the bone. Serve immediately.

Pork Chops with Mushroom-Tomato Sauce

Costolette di Maiale con Funghi

Makes 4 servings

When buying pork chops, look for chops of similar size and thickness so that they will cook evenly. White button mushrooms, wine, and tomatoes are the sauce for these pork chops. This same treatment is also good on veal chops.

4 tablespoons olive oil

4 center-cut pork loin chops, each about 1 inch thick

Salt and freshly ground black pepper

½ cup dry white wine

1 cup chopped fresh or canned tomatoes

1 tablespoon chopped fresh rosemary

1 (12-ounce) package white mushrooms, lightly rinsed, stemmed, and halved or quartered if large

1. In a large heavy skillet, heat 2 tablespoons of the oil over medium heat. Sprinkle the chops with salt and pepper. Place the chops in the pan in a single layer. Cook until they are nicely browned on one side, about 2 minutes. Turn the chops over with tongs and brown on the other side, about 1 to 2 minutes more. Transfer the chops to a plate.

2. Add the wine to the skillet and bring to a simmer. Add the tomatoes, rosemary, and salt and pepper to taste. Cover and cook 10 minutes.

3. Meanwhile, in a medium skillet, heat the remaining 2 tablespoons of oil over medium heat. Add the mushrooms, and salt and pepper to taste. Cook, stirring frequently, until the liquid evaporates and the mushrooms are browned, about 10 minutes.

4. Return the pork chops to the skillet with the tomato sauce. Stir in the mushrooms. Cover and cook 5 to 10 minutes more or until the pork is just cooked through and the sauce is slightly thickened. Serve immediately.

Pork Chops with Porcini and Red Wine

Costolette con Funghi e Vino

Makes 4 servings

Browning chops or other cuts of meat adds flavor and improves their appearance. Always pat the chops dry just before browning them, as surface moisture will cause the meat to steam and not brown. After browning, these chops are simmered with dried porcini and red wine. A touch of heavy cream gives the sauce a smooth texture and rich flavor.

1 ounce dried porcini mushrooms

1½ cups warm water

2 tablespoons olive oil

4 center-cut pork loin chops, about 1 inch thick

Salt and freshly ground black pepper

½ cup dry red wine

¼ cup heavy cream

1. Place the mushrooms in a bowl with the water. Let stand 30 minutes. Lift the mushrooms out of the liquid and rinse them well under running water, paying special attention to the base of the stems where soil collects. Drain, then chop fine. Pour the soaking liquid through a paper coffee filter–lined strainer into a bowl.

2. In a large skillet, heat the oil over medium heat. Pat the chops dry. Place the chops in the pan in a single layer. Cook until they are nicely browned, about 2 minutes. Turn the chops over with tongs and brown on the other side, about 1 to 2 minutes more. Sprinkle with salt and pepper. Transfer the chops to a plate.

3. Add the wine to the skillet and simmer 1 minute. Add the porcini and their soaking liquid. Reduce the heat to low. Simmer 5 to 10 minutes, or until the liquid is reduced. Stir in the cream and cook 5 minutes more.

4. Return the chops to the pan. Cook 5 minutes more, or until the chops are just cooked through and the sauce is thickened. Serve immediately.

Pork Chops with Cabbage

Costolette di Maiale con Cavolo Rosso

Makes 4 servings

Balsamic vinegar adds color and sweetness to red cabbage and offers a nice balance to the pork. It is not necessary to use an aged balsamic vinegar for this recipe. Save it to use as a condiment for cheese or cooked meat.

2 tablespoons olive oil

4 center-cut pork loin chops, about 1 inch thick

Salt and freshly ground black pepper

1 large onion, chopped

2 large garlic cloves, finely chopped

2 pounds red cabbage, cut into thin strips

¼ cup balsamic vinegar

2 tablespoons water

1. In a large skillet, heat the oil over medium heat. Pat the chops dry with paper towels. Add the chops to the pan. Cook until nicely browned, about 2 minutes. Turn the meat over with tongs and brown on the other side, about 1 to 2 minutes more. Sprinkle with salt and pepper. Transfer the chops to a plate.

2. Add the onion to the skillet and cook 5 minutes. Stir in the garlic and cook 1 minute more.

3. Add the cabbage, balsamic vinegar, water, and salt to taste. Cover and cook, stirring occasionally, until the cabbage is tender, about 45 minutes.

4. Add the chops to the pan and cook, turning the chops once or twice in the sauce, until the meat is just cooked through and slightly pink when cut near the bone, about 5 minutes more. Serve immediately.

Pork Chops with Fennel and White Wine

Braciole di Maiale al Vino

Makes 4 servings

There is not a lot of sauce left in the pan when these chops are done, just a tablespoon or two of concentrated glaze to moisten the meat. If you prefer not to use fennel seeds, try substituting a tablespoon of fresh rosemary.

2 tablespoons olive oil

4 center-cut pork loin chops, about 1 inch thick

1 garlic clove, lightly crushed

Salt and freshly ground black pepper

2 teaspoons fennel seeds

1 cup dry white wine

1. In a large skillet, heat the oil over medium-high heat. Pat the pork chops dry. Add the pork chops and garlic to the pan. Cook until the chops are browned, about 2 minutes. Sprinkle with the fennel seeds and the salt and pepper. Turn the chops over with tongs and brown on the second side, about 1 to 2 minutes more.

2. Add the wine and bring to a simmer. Cover and cook 3 to 5 minutes or until the chops are cooked through and just pink when cut near the bone.

3. Transfer the chops to a plate and discard the garlic. Cook the pan juices until reduced and syrupy. Pour the juices over the chops and serve immediately.

Pork Chops, Pizzamaker's Style

Braciole alla Pizzaiola

Makes 4 servings

In Naples, pork chops and small steaks, too, can be prepared alla pizzaiola, in the style of the pizzamaker. The sauce is typically served over spaghetti as a first course. The chops are served as a second course with a green salad. There should be just enough sauce for a half-pound of spaghetti, with a spoonful or so left to serve with the chops.

2 tablespoons olive oil

4 pork rib chops, about 1 inch thick

Salt and freshly ground black pepper

2 large garlic cloves, finely chopped

1 (28-ounce) can peeled tomatoes, drained and chopped

1 teaspoon dried oregano

Pinch crushed red pepper

2 tablespoons chopped fresh flat-leaf parsley

1. In a large skillet, heat the oil over medium heat. Pat the chops dry and sprinkle with salt and pepper. Add the chops to the pan. Cook until the chops are browned, about 2 minutes. Turn the chops over with tongs and brown on the other side, about 2 minutes more. Transfer the chops to a plate.

2. Add the garlic to the pan and cook 1 minute. Add the tomatoes, oregano, red pepper, and salt to taste. Bring the sauce to a simmer. Cook, stirring occasionally, 20 minutes or until the sauce is thickened.

3. Return the chops to the sauce. Cook 5 minutes, turning the chops once or twice, until they are just cooked through and slightly pink when cut near the bone. Sprinkle with parsley. Serve immediately, or if using the sauce for spaghetti, cover the chops with foil to keep warm.

Pork Chops, Molise Style

Pampanella Sammartinese

Makes 4 servings

These chops are spicy and unusual. At one time cooks in Molise would dry their own sweet red peppers in the sun to make paprika. Today, commercially made sweet paprika is used in Italy. In the United States, use paprika imported from Hungary for best flavor.

Grilling pork chops is tricky because they can dry out so easily. Watch them carefully and cook them only until the meat is just slightly pink near the bone.

¼ cup sweet paprika

2 garlic cloves, chopped

1 teaspoon salt

Crushed red pepper

2 tablespoons white wine vinegar

4 center-cut pork loin chops, about 1 inch thick

1. In a small bowl, mix together the paprika, garlic, salt, and a generous pinch of crushed red pepper. Add the vinegar and stir until smooth. Place the chops on a plate and brush them on all sides with the paste. Cover and refrigerate 1 hour up to overnight.

2. Place a barbecue grill or broiler rack about 6 inches from the heat source. Preheat the grill or broiler. Cook pork chops until browned on one side, about 6 minutes, then turn the meat over with tongs and brown the other side, about 5 minutes more. Cut into the chops near the bone; the meat should be slightly pink. Serve immediately.

Balsamic-Glazed Pork Tenderloin with Arugula and Parmigiano

Maiale al Balsamico con Insalata

Makes 6 servings

Pork tenderloins are quick-cooking and low in fat. Here, the glazed pork slices are paired with a crisp arugula salad. If you cannot find arugula, substitute watercress.

2 pork tenderloins (about 1 pound each)

1 garlic clove, finely chopped

1 tablespoon balsamic vinegar

1 teaspoon honey

Salt and freshly ground black pepper

Salad

2 tablespoons olive oil

1 tablespoon balsamic vinegar

Salt and freshly ground black pepper

6 cups trimmed arugula, rinsed and dried

A piece of Parmigiano-Reggiano

1. Place a rack in the center of the oven. Preheat the oven to 450°F. Oil a baking pan just large enough to hold the pork.

2. Pat the pork dry with paper towels. Fold the thin ends under to make it an even thickness. Place the tenderloins about an inch apart in the pan.

3. In a small bowl, stir together the garlic, vinegar, honey, and salt and pepper to taste.

4. Brush the mixture over the meat. Place the pork in the oven and roast 15 minutes. Pour $1/2$ cup of water around the meat. Roast 10 to 20 minutes more or until browned and tender. (Pork is done when the internal temperature reaches 150°F on an instant-read thermometer.) Remove the pork from the oven. Leave it in the pan and let it rest at least 10 minutes.

5. In a large bowl, whisk together the oil, vinegar, and salt and pepper to taste. Add the arugula and toss with the dressing. Pile the arugula in the center of a large platter or individual dinner plates.

6. Thinly slice the pork and arrange it around the greens. Drizzle with the pan juices. With a swivel-blade vegetable peeler, shave thin slices of Parmigiano-Reggiano over the arugula. Serve immediately.

Herbed Pork Tenderloin

Filetto di Maiale alle Erbe

Makes 6 servings

Pork tenderloins are now readily available, usually packed two to a package. They are lean and tender, if not overcooked, though the flavor is very mild. Grilling gives them added flavor, and they can be served hot or at room temperature.

2 pork tenderloins (about 1 pound each)

2 tablespoons olive oil

2 tablespoons chopped fresh sage

2 tablespoons chopped fresh basil

2 tablespoons chopped fresh rosemary

1 garlic clove, finely chopped

Salt and freshly ground black pepper

1. Pat the meat dry with paper towels. Place the pork tenderloins on a plate.

2. In a small bowl, mix together the oil, herbs, garlic, and salt and pepper to taste. Rub the mixture over the tenderloins. Cover and refrigerate at least 1 hour or up to overnight.

3. Preheat the grill or broiler. Grill the tenderloins 7 to 10 minutes, or until browned. Turn the meat over with tongs and cook 7 minutes more, or until an instant-read thermometer inserted in the center reads 150°F. Sprinkle with salt. Let the meat rest 10 minutes before slicing. Serve hot or at room temperature.

Calabrian-Style Pork Tenderloin with Honey and Chile

Carne 'ncantarata

Makes 6 servings

More than any other region in Italy, cooks in Calabria incorporate chile peppers into their cooking. Chiles are used fresh, dried, ground, or crushed into flakes or powder—as paprika or cayenne.

In Castrovillari, my husband and I ate at the Locanda di Alia, an elegant country restaurant and inn. The region's most famous restaurant is run by the Alia brothers. Gaetano is the chef, while Pinuccio manages the front of the house. Their specialty is pork marinated with fennel and chiles in a honey and chile sauce. Pinuccio explained that the recipe, which is at least two hundred years old, was made with preserved pork that had been salted and cured for several months. This is a more streamlined way of making it.

Fennel pollen can be found at many shops specializing in herbs and spices. (See Sources.) Crushed fennel seeds can be used if the pollen is not available.

2 pork tenderloins (about 1 pound each)

2 tablespoons honey

1 teaspoon salt

1 teaspoon fennel pollen or crushed fennel seeds

Pinch of crushed red pepper

½ cup orange juice

2 tablespoons paprika

1. Place a rack in the center of the oven. Preheat the oven to 425°F. Oil a baking pan just large enough to hold the pork.

2. Fold the thin ends of the tenderloins under to make an even thickness. Place the tenderloins about an inch apart in the pan.

3. In a small bowl, stir together the honey, salt, fennel pollen, and crushed red pepper. Brush the mixture over the meat. Place the pork in the oven and roast 15 minutes.

4. Pour the orange juice around the meat. Roast 10 to 20 minutes more, or until browned and tender. (Pork is done when the internal temperature reaches 150°F on an instant-read

thermometer.) Transfer the pork to a cutting board. Cover with foil and keep warm while preparing the sauce.

5. Place the baking pan over medium heat. Stir in the paprika and cook, scraping the bottom of the pan, for 2 minutes.

6. Slice the pork and serve it with the sauce.

Roast Pork with Potatoes and Rosemary

Arista di Maiale con Patate

Makes 6 to 8 servings

Everybody loves this pork roast—it's easy to make, and the potatoes absorb the flavors of the pork as they cook together in the same pan. Irresistible.

1 center-cut boneless pork loin roast (about 3 pounds)

2 tablespoons chopped fresh rosemary

2 tablespoons chopped fresh garlic

4 tablespoons olive oil

Salt and freshly ground black pepper

2 pounds new potatoes, halved, or quartered if large

1. Place a rack in the center of the oven. Preheat the oven to 425°F. Oil a roasting pan large enough to hold the pork and potatoes without crowding.

2. In a small bowl, make a paste with the rosemary, garlic, 2 tablespoons of the oil, and a generous amount of salt and

pepper. Toss the potatoes in the pan with the remaining 2 tablespoons of oil and half of the garlic paste. Push the potatoes aside and place the meat fat-side up in the center of the pan. Rub or spread the remaining paste all over the meat.

3. Roast 20 minutes. Turn the potatoes. Reduce the heat to 350°F. Roast 1 hour more, turning the potatoes every 20 minutes. The meat is done when the internal temperature of the pork reaches 150°F on an instant-read thermometer.

4. Transfer the meat to a cutting board. Cover loosely with foil and let rest 10 minutes. The potatoes should be browned and tender. If necessary, turn up the heat and cook them a little more.

5. Slice the meat and arrange it on a warm serving platter surrounded by the potatoes. Serve hot.

Pork Loin with Lemon

Maiale con Limone

Makes 6 to 8 servings

Pork loin roasted with lemon zest makes a fine Sunday dinner. I serve it with slow-cooked cannellini beans and a green vegetable like broccoli or brussels sprouts.

Butterflying the loin is easy enough to do yourself if you follow the instructions; otherwise have the butcher handle it.

1 center-cut boneless pork loin roast (about 3 pounds)

1 teaspoon grated lemon zest

2 garlic cloves, finely chopped

2 tablespoons chopped fresh flat-leaf parsley

2 tablespoons olive oil

Salt and freshly ground black pepper

½ cup dry white wine

1. Place a rack in the center of the oven. Preheat the oven to 425°F. Oil a roasting pan just large enough to hold the meat.

2. In a small bowl, mix together the lemon zest, garlic, parsley, oil, and salt and pepper to taste.

3. Pat the meat dry with paper towels. To butterfly the pork, place it on a cutting board. With a long sharp knife such as a boning knife or chef's knife, cut the pork almost in half lengthwise, stopping about 3/4 inch from one long side. Open the meat like a book. Spread the lemon and garlic mixture over the side of the meat. Roll up the pork from one long side to the other like a sausage and tie it with kitchen string at 2-inch intervals. Sprinkle the outside with salt and pepper.

4. Place the meat fat-side up in the prepared pan. Roast 20 minutes. Reduce the heat to 350°F. Roast 40 minutes more. Add the wine and roast 15 to 30 minutes longer, or until the temperature on an instant-read thermometer reaches 150°F.

5. Transfer the roast to a cutting board. Cover the meat loosely with foil. Let rest 10 minutes before slicing. Place the pan on the stove over medium heat and reduce the pan juices slightly. Slice the pork and transfer it to a serving platter. Pour the juices over the meat. Serve hot.

Pork Loin with Apples and Grappa

Maiale con Mele

Makes 6 to 8 servings

Apples and onions teamed with grappa and rosemary flavor this tasty roast pork loin from Friuli–Venezia Giulia.

1 center-cut boneless pork loin roast (about 3 pounds)

1 tablespoon chopped fresh rosemary, plus more for garnish

Salt and freshly ground black pepper

2 tablespoons olive oil

2 Granny Smith or other tart apples, peeled and thinly sliced

1 small onion, thinly sliced

¼ cup grappa or brandy

½ cup dry white wine

1. Place a rack in the center of the oven. Preheat the oven to 350°F. Lightly oil a roasting pan large enough to hold the meat.

2. Rub the pork with the rosemary, salt and pepper to taste, and olive oil. Place the meat fat-side up in the pan and surround it with the apple and onion slices.

3. Pour the grappa and wine over the meat. Roast for 1 hour and 15 minutes, or until an instant-read thermometer inserted in the center reads 150°F. Transfer the meat to a cutting board and cover with foil to keep warm.

4. The apples and onions should be soft. If not, return the pan to the oven and roast 15 minutes more.

5. When they are tender, scrape the apples and onions into a food processor or blender. Puree until smooth. (Add a tablespoon or two of warm water to thin the mixture if needed.)

6. Slice the meat and arrange it on a heated platter. Spoon the apple-onion puree to one side. Garnish with fresh rosemary. Serve hot.

Roast Pork with Hazelnuts and Cream

Arrosto di Maiale alle Nocciole

Makes 6 to 8 servings

This is a variation on a Piedmontese roast pork recipe that first appeared in my book Italian Holiday Cooking. Here cream, along with hazelnuts, enriches the sauce.

1 center-cut boneless pork loin roast (about 3 pounds)

2 tablespoons chopped fresh rosemary

2 large garlic cloves, finely chopped

2 tablespoons olive oil

Salt and freshly ground black pepper

1 cup dry white wine

½ cup hazelnuts, toasted, skinned, and coarsely chopped (see How To Toast and Skin Nuts)

1 cup homemade Meat Broth or Chicken Broth, or store-bought beef or chicken broth

½ cup heavy cream

1. Place a rack in the center of the oven. Preheat the oven to 425°F. Oil a roasting pan just large enough to hold the meat.

2. In a small bowl, mix together the rosemary, garlic, oil, and salt and pepper to taste. Place the meat fat-side up in the pan. Rub the garlic mixture all over the pork. Roast the meat 15 minutes.

3. Pour the wine over the meat. Cook 45 to 60 minutes more, or until the temperature of the pork reaches 150°F on an instant-read thermometer and the meat is tender when pierced with a fork. Meanwhile, prepare the hazelnuts, if necessary.

4. Transfer the meat to a cutting board. Cover with foil to keep warm.

5. Place the pan over medium heat on the top of the stove and bring the juices to a simmer. Add the broth and simmer 5 minutes, scraping up and blending in the browned bits on the bottom of the pan with a wooden spoon. Add the cream and simmer until slightly thickened, about 2 minutes more. Stir in the chopped nuts and remove from the heat.

6. Slice the meat and arrange the slices on a warm serving platter. Spoon the sauce over the pork and serve hot.

Tuscan Pork Loin

Arista di Maiale

Makes 6 to 8 servings

Here is a classic Tuscan-style pork roast. Cooking the meat with the bone makes it much more flavorful, and the bones are also great to gnaw on.

3 large garlic cloves

2 tablespoons fresh rosemary

Salt and freshly ground black pepper

2 tablespoons olive oil

1 bone-in center-cut rib roast, about 4 pounds

1 cup dry white wine

1. Place a rack in the center of the oven. Preheat the oven to 325°F. Oil a roasting pan just large enough to hold the roast.

2. Very finely chop the garlic and rosemary together, then place them in a small bowl. Add the salt and pepper to taste and mix well to form a paste. Place the roast fat-side up in the pan. With a

small knife, make deep slits all over the surface of the pork, then insert the mixture into the slits. Rub the roast all over with the olive oil.

3. Roast 1 hour 15 minutes or until the meat reaches an internal temperature of 150°F on an instant-read thermometer. Transfer the meat to a cutting board. Cover with foil to keep warm. Let rest 10 minutes.

4. Place the pan over low heat on the top of the stove. Add the wine and cook, scraping up and blending in the browned bits at the bottom of the pan with a wooden spoon until slightly reduced, about 2 minutes. Pour the juices through a strainer into a bowl and skim off the fat. Reheat if necessary.

5. Slice the meat and arrange it on a warm serving platter. Serve it hot with the pan juices.

Roast Pork Shoulder with Fennel

Porchetta

Makes 12 servings

This is my version of the fabulous roast pig known as porchetta, sold all around central Italy, including Lazio, Umbria, and Abruzzo. Slices of the pork are sold from special trucks, and you can order it on a sandwich or wrapped in paper to take home. Though the meat is luscious, the crackling pork skin is the best part.

The roast is cooked for a long time and to a high temperature because it is very dense. The high fat content keeps the meat moist, and the skin gets brown and crunchy. A fresh ham can be substituted for the pork shoulder.

1 (7-pound) pork shoulder roast

8 to 12 garlic cloves

2 tablespoons chopped fresh rosemary

1 tablespoon fennel seeds

1 tablespoon salt

1 teaspoon freshly ground black pepper

¼ cup olive oil

1. About 1 hour before you begin roasting the meat, remove it from the refrigerator.

2. Very finely chop together the garlic, rosemary, fennel, and salt, then place the seasonings in a small bowl. Stir in the pepper and oil to form a smooth paste.

3. With a small knife, cut deep slits into the surface of the pork. Insert the paste into the slits.

4. Place a rack in the lower third of the oven. Preheat the oven to 350°F. When ready, place the roast in the oven and cook 3 hours. Spoon off the excess fat. Roast the meat 1 to 1½ hours longer, or until the temperature reaches 160°F on an instant-read thermometer. When the meat is done, the fat will be crisp and a deep nutty brown.

5. Transfer the meat to a cutting board. Cover with foil to keep warm and let stand 20 minutes. Carve and serve hot or at room temperature.

Roast Suckling Pig

Maialino Arrosto

Makes 8 to 10 servings

A suckling pig is one that has not been allowed to eat adult pig food. In the United States, suckling pigs typically weigh between 15 and 20 pounds, though in Italy they are half that size. Even at the higher weight, there really is not much meat on a suckling pig, so don't plan to serve more than eight to ten guests. Also, be sure you have a very large baking pan to accommodate a whole piglet, which will be about 30 inches long, and be sure your oven will accommodate the pan. Any good butcher should be able to obtain a fresh piglet for you, but make inquiries before planning on it.

Sardinian cooks are famous for their suckling pig, but I have eaten it in many places in Italy. The one I remember best was part of a memorable luncheon enjoyed at the Majo di Norante winery in Abruzzo.

1 suckling pig, about 15 pounds

4 garlic cloves

2 tablespoons chopped fresh flat-leaf parsley

1 tablespoon chopped fresh rosemary

1 tablespoon chopped fresh sage

1 teaspoon juniper berries, chopped

Salt and freshly ground black pepper

6 tablespoons olive oil

2 bay leaves

1 cup dry white wine

Apple, orange, or other fruit for garnish (optional)

1. Place a rack in the lower third of the oven. Preheat the oven to 425°F. Oil a baking pan large enough to hold the pig.

2. Rinse the pig well inside and out and pat dry with paper towels.

3. Chop together the garlic, parsley, rosemary, sage, and juniper berries, then place the seasonings in a small bowl. Add a generous amount of salt and freshly ground pepper. Stir in two tablespoons of the oil.

4. Place the pig on its side on a large roasting rack in the prepared pan and spread the herb mixture inside the body cavity. Add the bay leaves. Cut slashes about 1/2 inch deep along both sides of the backbone. Rub the remaining oil all over the surface of the pig. Cover the ears and tail with aluminum foil. (If you want to serve the pig whole with an apple or other fruit in its mouth, prop the mouth open with a ball of aluminum foil about the size of the fruit.) Sprinkle the outside with salt and pepper.

5. Roast the pig 30 minutes. Reduce the heat to 350°F. Baste with the wine. Roast 2 to 2^1/$_2$ hours more, or until an instant-read thermometer inserted in the meaty part of the hindquarter registers 170°F. Baste every 20 minutes with the pan juices.

6. Transfer the pig to a large cutting board. Cover with foil and let rest 30 minutes. Remove the foil covering and the ball of foil from the mouth, if using. Replace the foil ball with the fruit, if using. Transfer to a serving platter and serve hot.

7. Skim the fat from the pan juices and reheat them over low heat. Pour the juices over the meat. Serve immediately.

Boneless Spiced Pork Loin Roast

Maiale in Porchetta

Makes 6 to 8 servings

Boneless pork loin is roasted with the same spices used for porchetta (baby pig roasted on a spit) in many parts of central Italy. After a brief period of cooking at high heat, the oven temperature is turned down low, which keeps the meat tender and juicy.

4 garlic cloves

1 tablespoon fresh rosemary

6 fresh sage leaves

6 juniper berries

1 teaspoon salt

½ teaspoon freshly ground black pepper

1 boneless center-cut pork loin roast, about 3 pounds

Extra-virgin olive oil

1 cup dry white wine

1. Place a rack in the center of the oven. Preheat the oven to 450°F. Oil a roasting pan just large enough to hold the pork.

2. Very finely chop together the garlic, rosemary, sage, and juniper berries. Stir together the herb mixture, the salt, and the pepper.

3. With a large, sharp knife, cut the meat lengthwise down the center, leaving it attached on one side. Open the meat like a book and spread two-thirds of the spice mixture over the meat. Close the meat and tie it with string at 2-inch intervals. Rub the remaining spice mixture over the outside. Place the meat in the pan. Drizzle with olive oil.

4. Roast the pork 10 minutes. Reduce the heat to 300°F and roast 60 minutes more, or until the internal temperature of the pork reaches 150°F.

5. Remove the roast to a serving platter and cover with foil. Let rest 10 minutes.

6. Add the wine to the pan and place it over medium heat on the top of the stove. Cook, scraping up any brown bits in the pan with a wooden spoon, until the juices are reduced and syrupy. Slice the pork and spoon on the pan juices. Serve hot.

Braised Pork Shoulder in Milk

Maiale al Latte

Makes 6 to 8 servings

In Lombardy and the Veneto, veal, pork, and chicken are sometimes cooked in milk. This keeps the meat tender, and when it is done the milk makes a creamy brown sauce to serve with the meat.

Vegetables, pancetta, and wine add flavor. I use a boneless shoulder or butt roast for this dish because it takes well to slow, moist cooking. The meat is cooked on the stove, so you don't need to turn on your oven.

1 boneless pork shoulder or butt roast (about 3 pounds)

4 ounces finely diced pancetta

1 carrot, finely chopped

1 small tender celery rib

1 medium onion, finely chopped

1 quart milk

Salt and freshly ground black pepper

½ cup dry white wine

1. In a large Dutch oven or other deep, heavy pot with a tight-fitting lid, combine the pork, pancetta, carrot, celery, onion, milk, and salt and pepper to taste. Bring the liquid to a simmer over medium heat.

2. Partially cover the pot and cook over medium heat, turning occasionally, about 2 hours or until the meat is tender when pierced with a fork.

3. Transfer the meat to a cutting board. Cover with foil to keep warm. Raise the heat under the pot and cook until the liquid is reduced and lightly browned. Pour the juices through a strainer into a bowl, then pour the liquid back into the pot

4. Pour the wine into the pot and bring to a simmer, scraping up and blending in any browned bits with a wooden spoon. Slice the pork and arrange it on a warm serving platter. Pour the cooking liquid over the top. Serve hot.

Braised Pork Shoulder with Grapes

Maiale all' Uva

Makes 6 to 8 servings

Pork shoulder or butt is particularly good for braising. It stays nice and moist despite the long simmering. I used to make this Sicilian recipe with pork loin, but I now find that the loin is too lean and shoulder has more flavor.

1 pound pearl onions

3 pounds boneless pork shoulder or butt, rolled and tied

2 tablespoons olive oil

Salt and freshly ground black pepper

¼ cup white wine vinegar

1 pound **seedless green grapes**, stemmed (about 3 cups)

1. Bring a large pot of water to a boil. Add the onions and cook for 30 seconds. Drain and cool under cold running water.

2. With a sharp paring knife, shave off the tip of the root ends. Do not slice off the ends too deeply or the onions will fall apart during cooking. Remove the skins.

3. In a Dutch oven just large enough to hold the meat or another deep, heavy pot with a tight-fitting lid, heat the oil over medium-high heat. Pat the pork dry with paper towels. Place the pork in the pot and brown well on all sides, about 20 minutes. Tip the pot and spoon off the fat. Sprinkle the pork with salt and pepper.

4. Add the vinegar and bring it to a simmer, scraping up the browned bits at the bottom of the pot with a wooden spoon. Add the onions and 1 cup water. Reduce the heat to low and simmer 1 hour.

5. Add the grapes. Cook 30 minutes more or until the meat is very tender when pierced with a fork. Transfer the meat to a cutting board. Cover with foil to keep warm and let sit 15 minutes.

6. Slice the pork and arrange it on a warm serving platter. Spoon on the grape and onion sauce and serve immediately.

Beer-Braised Pork Shoulder

Maiale alla Birra

Makes 8 servings

Fresh pork shanks are cooked this way in Trentino– Alto Adige, but since that cut is not widely available in the United States, I use the same flavorings to cook a bone-in shoulder roast. There will be a lot of fat at the end of the cooking time, but this can easily be skimmed off the surface of the cooking liquid. Better yet, cook the pork a day ahead of serving and chill the meat and cooking juices separately. The fat will harden and can easily be removed. Reheat the pork in the cooking liquid before serving.

5 to 7 pounds bone-in pork shoulder (picnic or Boston butt)

Salt and freshly ground black pepper

2 tablespoons olive oil

1 medium onion, finely chopped

2 garlic cloves, finely chopped

2 sprigs fresh rosemary

2 bay leaves

12 ounces beer

1. Pat the pork dry with paper towels. Sprinkle the meat all over with salt and pepper.

2. In a large Dutch oven or other deep, heavy pot with a tight-fitting lid, heat the oil over medium heat. Place the pork in the pot and brown it well on all sides, about 20 minutes Spoon off all but 1 or 2 tablespoons of the fat.

3. Scatter the onion, garlic, rosemary, and bay leaves all around the meat and cook 5 minutes. Add the beer and bring to a simmer.

4. Cover the pot and cook, turning the meat occasionally, for $2^1/_2$ to 3 hours, or until the meat is tender when pierced with a knife.

5. Strain the pan juices and skim off the fat. Slice the pork and serve it with the pan juices. Serve hot.

Lamb Chops with White Wine

Braciole di Agnello al Vino Bianco

Makes 4 servings

Here is a basic way of preparing lamb chops that can be made with either tender loin or rib cuts or chewier, but much less expensive, shoulder chops. For best flavor, trim the meat of excess fat and cook the chops just until pink in the center.

2 tablespoons olive oil

8 loin or rib lamb chops, 1 inch thick, trimmed

4 garlic cloves, lightly crushed

3 or 4 (2-inch) rosemary sprigs

Salt and freshly ground black pepper

1 cup dry white wine

1. In a skillet large enough to hold the chops comfortably in a single layer, heat the oil over medium-high heat. When the oil is hot, pat the chops dry. Sprinkle the chops with salt and pepper, then place them in the pan. Cook until the chops are browned, about 4 minutes. Scatter the garlic and rosemary around the meat. Using tongs, turn the chops and brown on the other side, about 3 minutes. Transfer the chops to a plate.

2. Add the wine to the skillet and bring to a simmer. Cook, scraping up and blending in the browned bits in the bottom of the pan, until the wine is reduced and slightly thickened, about 2 minutes.

3. Return the chops to the pan and cook them 2 minutes more, turning them in the sauce once or twice until rosy pink when cut near the bone. Transfer the chops to a platter, pour the pan juices over the chops, and serve immediately.

Lamb Chops with Capers, Lemon, and Sage

Braciole di Agnello con Capperi

Makes 4 servings

Vecchia Roma is one of my favorite Roman restaurants. On the fringe of the old ghetto, it has a beautiful outdoor garden for eating when the weather is warm and sunny, but I also enjoy the cozy inside dining rooms when it is cold or rainy. This lamb is inspired by a dish I tasted there made with tiny nuggets of baby lamb. I have adapted it to tender chops instead, because they are widely available here.

1 tablespoon olive oil

8 loin or rib lamb chops, 1 inch thick, trimmed

Salt and freshly ground black pepper

½ cup dry white wine

3 tablespoons fresh lemon juice

3 tablespoons capers, rinsed and chopped

6 fresh sage leaves

1. In a large skillet, heat the oil over medium-high heat. Pat the chops dry. When the oil is hot, sprinkle them with salt and pepper, then place chops in the pan. Cook until the chops are browned, about 4 minutes. Using tongs, turn the chops and brown on the other side, about 3 minutes. Transfer the chops to a plate.

2. Pour the fat out of the pan. Reduce the heat to low. Stir the wine, the lemon juice, capers, and sage into the pan. Bring to a simmer and cook 2 minutes or until slightly syrupy.

3. Return the chops to the pan and turn them once or twice until heated through and just pink when cut near the bone. Serve immediately.

Lamb Chops in Crispy Coating

Braciolette Croccante

Makes 4 servings

In Milan, I ate goat meat chops prepared this way, accompanied by artichoke hearts fried in the same crispy coating. Romans use tiny lamb chops instead of goat and leave out the cheese. Either way, a crisp mixed salad is the perfect accompaniment.

8 to 12 rib lamb chops, about ¾ inch thick, well trimmed

2 large eggs

Salt and freshly ground black pepper

1¼ cups plain dry bread crumbs

½ cup freshly grated Parmigiano-Reggiano

Olive oil for frying

1. Place the chops on a cutting board and gently pound the meat to about a $1/2$-inch thickness.

2. In a shallow plate, beat the eggs with salt and pepper to taste. Toss the bread crumbs with the cheese on a sheet of wax paper.

3. Dip the chops one at a time in the eggs, then roll them in the bread crumbs, patting the crumbs in well.

4. Turn the oven on to the lowest setting. Pour about $1/2$ inch of the oil into a deep skillet. Heat the oil over medium-high heat until a little of the egg mixture cooks quickly when dropped in the oil. With tongs, carefully place a few of the chops in the oil without crowding the pan. Cook until browned and crisp, 3 to 4 minutes. Turn the chops with tongs and brown, 3 minutes. Drain the chops on paper towels. Keep the fried chops warm in the oven while frying the remainder. Serve hot.

Lamb Chops with Artichokes and Olives

Costolette di Agnello ai Carciofi e Olive

Makes 4 servings

All of the ingredients of this dish cook in the same skillet so that the complementary flavors of the lamb, artichokes, and olives blend smoothly. A bright vegetable like carrots or baked tomatoes would be a good accompaniment.

2 tablespoons olive oil

8 rib or loin lamb chops, about 1 inch thick, trimmed

Salt and freshly ground black pepper to taste

2 tablespoons olive oil

¾ cup dry white wine

8 small or 4 medium artichokes, trimmed and cut into eighths

1 garlic clove, finely chopped

½ cup small mild black olives, such as Gaeta

1 tablespoon chopped fresh flat-leaf parsley

1. In a skillet large enough to hold the chops in a single layer, heat the oil over medium heat. Pat the lamb dry. When the oil is hot, sprinkle the chops with salt and pepper, then place them in the pan. Cook until the chops are browned, 3 to 4 minutes. Using tongs, turn the chops to brown on the other side, about 3 minutes. Transfer the chops to a plate.

2. Turn the heat to medium-low. Add the wine and bring to a simmer. Cook 1 minute. Add the artichokes, garlic, and salt and pepper to taste. Cover the pan and cook 20 minutes or until the artichokes are tender.

3. Stir in the olives and parsley and cook 1 minute more. Return the chops to the pan and cook, turning the lamb once or twice until heated through. Serve immediately.

Lamb Chops with Tomato, Caper, and Anchovy Sauce

Costelette d'Agnello in Salsa

Makes 4 servings

A spicy tomato sauce flavors these Calabrese-style chops. Pork chops can also be cooked this way.

2 tablespoons olive oil

8 rib or loin lamb chops, about ¾ inch thick, trimmed

6 to 8 plum tomatoes, peeled, seeded, and chopped

4 anchovy fillets, chopped

1 tablespoon capers, rinsed and chopped

2 tablespoons chopped fresh flat-leaf parsley

1. In a skillet large enough to hold the chops comfortably in a single layer, heat the oil over medium heat. When the oil is hot, pat the chops dry. Sprinkle the chops with salt and pepper, then add the chops to the pan. Cook until the chops are browned,

about 4 minutes. Using tongs, turn the chops and brown on the other side, about 3 minutes. Transfer the chops to a plate.

2. Add the tomatoes, anchovies, and capers to the pan. Add a pinch of salt and pepper to taste. Cook 5 minutes or until slightly thickened.

3. Return the chops to the pan and cook, turning them once or twice in the sauce until heated through and pink when cut near the bone. Sprinkle with parsley and serve immediately.

"Burn-the-Fingers" Lamb Chops

Agnello a Scottadito

Makes 4 servings

In the recipe that inspired this dish, from an old cookbook on Umbrian cuisine, finely chopped prosciutto fat flavors the lamb. Most cooks today substitute olive oil. Lamb riblets are also good this way.

Presumably the name comes from the idea that the chops are so delicious you can't help but eat them right away—hot, right off the grill or out of the pan.

¼ cup olive oil

2 garlic cloves, finely chopped

1 tablespoon chopped fresh rosemary

1 teaspoon chopped fresh thyme

8 rib lamb chops, about 1 inch thick, trimmed

Salt and freshly ground black pepper

1. In a small bowl, stir together the oil, garlic, herbs, and salt and pepper to taste. Brush the mixture over the lamb. Cover and refrigerate 1 hour.

2. Place a grill or broiler rack about 5 inches away from the heat source. Preheat the grill or broiler.

3. Scrape off some of the marinade. Grill or broil the chops until browned and crisp, about 5 minutes. With tongs, turn the chops over and cook until browned and just pink in the center, about 5 minutes more. Serve hot.

Grilled Lamb, Basilicata Style

Agnello allo Spiedo

Makes 4 servings

Basilicata may be best known by its portrayal in Carlo Levi's Christ Stopped at Eboli. The author painted a bleak portrait of the region before World War II, when many political prisoners were sent there in exile. Today Basilicata, though still sparsely populated, is thriving, with many tourists venturing there for the beautiful beaches near Maratea.

Pork and lamb are typical meats in this region, and the two are combined in this recipe. The pancetta wrapping around the lamb cubes gets crisp and tasty. It keeps the lamb moist and adds flavor as it grills.

1½ pounds boneless leg of lamb, cut into 2-inch chunks

2 garlic cloves, finely chopped

1 tablespoon chopped fresh rosemary

Salt and freshly ground black pepper

4 ounces thinly sliced pancetta

¼ cup olive oil

2 tablespoons red wine vinegar

1. Place a barbecue grill or broiler rack about 5 inches away from the heat source. Preheat the grill or broiler.

2. In a large bowl, toss the lamb with the garlic, rosemary, and salt and pepper to taste.

3. Unroll the pancetta slices. Wrap a slice of pancetta around each chunk of lamb.

4. Thread the lamb on wooden skewers, securing the pancetta in place with the skewer. Place the pieces close together without crowding. In a small bowl, whisk together the oil and vinegar. Brush the mixture over the lamb.

5. Grill or broil the skewers, turning them occasionally, until done to taste—5 to 6 minutes for medium-rare. Serve hot.

Grilled Lamb Skewers

Arrosticini

Makes 4 servings

In Abruzzo, small bites of lamb are marinated, threaded on wooden skewers, and grilled over a hot fire. The cooked skewers are served standing in a tall cup or jug, and everyone helps themselves, eating the lamb right off the sticks. They are great for a buffet, served with roasted or sautéed peppers.

2 garlic cloves

Salt

1 pound lamb from the leg, trimmed and cut into ¾-inch chunks

3 tablesoons extra-virgin olive oil

2 tablespoons chopped fresh mint

1 teaspoon chopped fresh thyme

Freshly ground black pepper

1. Chop the garlic very fine. Sprinkle the garlic with a pinch of salt and mash it with the side of a large heavy chef's knife into a fine paste.

2. In a large bowl, toss the lamb with the garlic paste, oil, herbs, and salt and pepper to taste. Cover and marinate at room temperature for 1 hour or in the refrigerator for several hours or overnight.

3. Place a barbecue grill or broiler rack about 5 inches from the heat source. Preheat the grill or broiler.

4. Thread the meat on the skewers. Place the pieces close together without crowding. Grill or broil the lamb 3 minutes or until browned. Turn the meat over with tongs and cook 2 to 3 minutes more or until browned on the outside but still pink in the center. Serve hot.

Lamb Stew with Rosemary, Mint, and White Wine

Agnello in Umido

Makes 4 servings

Lamb shoulder is ideal for stewing. The meat has enough moisture to stand up to long, slow cooking, and though tough if cooked rare, it turns out fork-tender in a stew. If only bone-in lamb shoulder is available, it can be adapted to stewing recipes. Figure on an extra pound or two of bone-in meat, depending on just how bony it is. Cook bone-in lamb about 30 minutes longer than boneless, or until the meat is coming away from the bones.

2½ pounds boneless lamb shoulder, cut into 2-inch chunks

¼ cup olive oil

Salt and freshly ground black pepper to taste

1 large onion, chopped

4 garlic cloves, chopped

2 tablespoons chopped fresh rosemary

2 tablespoons chopped fresh flat-leaf parsley

1 tablespoon chopped fresh mint

½ cup dry white wine

About ½ cup beef broth (Meat Broth) or water

2 tablespoons tomato paste

1. In a large Dutch oven or other deep, heavy pot with a tight-fitting lid, heat the oil over medium heat. Dry the lamb with paper towels. Put just as many lamb pieces as will fit comfortably in a single layer into the pot. Cook, stirring frequently, until browned on all sides, about 20 minutes. Transfer the browned lamb to a plate. Sprinkle with salt and pepper. Cook the remaining lamb in the same way.

2. When all the meat is browned, spoon off the excess fat. Add the onion, garlic, and herbs and stir well. Cook until the onion has wilted, about 5 minutes.

3. Add the wine and bring to a simmer, scraping up and blending in the browned bits on the bottom of the pot. Cook 1 minute.

4. Add the broth and tomato paste. Reduce heat to low. Cover and cook 1 hour, stirring occasionally, or until the lamb is tender. Add a little water if the sauce becomes too dry. Serve hot.

Umbrian Lamb Stew with Chickpea Puree

Agnello del Colle

Makes 6 servings

Polenta and mashed potatoes are frequent accompaniments to stews in Italy, so I was surprised when this stew was served with mashed chickpeas in Umbria. Canned chickpeas work just fine, or you can cook dried chickpeas in advance.

2 tablespoons olive oil

3 pounds boneless lamb shoulder, cut into 2-inch chunks

Salt and freshly ground black pepper

2 garlic cloves, finely chopped

1 cup dry white wine

1½ cups chopped fresh or canned tomatoes

1 (10-ounce) package white mushrooms, sliced

2 (16-ounce) cans chickpeas or 5 cups cooked chickpeas

Extra-virgin olive oil

1. In a large Dutch oven or other deep, heavy pot with a tight-fitting lid, heat the oil over medium heat. Put just enough lamb pieces in the pot as will fit comfortably in a single layer. Cook, stirring occasionally, until browned on all sides, about 20 minutes. Transfer the browned lamb to a plate. Sprinkle with salt and pepper. Cook the remaining lamb in the same way.

2. When all of the meat is browned, spoon the excess fat from the pan. Scatter the garlic in the pan and cook 1 minute. Add the wine. With a wooden spoon, scrape up and blend in to the browned bits in the bottom of the pan. Bring to a simmer and cook 1 minute.

3. Return the lamb to the pot. Add the tomatoes and mushrooms and bring to a simmer. Reduce heat to low. Cover and cook, stirring occasionally, $1^1/_2$ hours or until the lamb is tender and the sauce is reduced. If there is too much liquid, remove the cover for the last 15 minutes.

4. Just before serving, heat the chickpeas and their liquid in a medium saucepan. Then transfer them to a food processor to puree or mash them with a potato masher. Stir in a little extra-virgin olive oil and black pepper to taste. Reheat if necessary.

5. To serve, scoop some of the chickpeas onto each plate. Surround the puree with the lamb stew. Serve hot.

Hunter's-Style Lamb

Agnello alla Cacciatora

Makes 6 to 8 servings

Romans make this lamb stew with abbacchio, lamb so young that it has never eaten grass. I think the flavor of mature lamb is a better match for the zesty chopped rosemary, vinegar, garlic, and anchovy that finish the sauce.

4 pounds bone-in lamb shoulder, cut into 2-inch chunks

Salt and freshly ground black pepper

2 tablespoons olive oil

4 garlic cloves, chopped

4 fresh sage leaves

2 (2-inch) sprigs fresh rosemary

1 cup dry white wine

6 anchovy fillets

1 teaspoon finely chopped fresh rosemary leaves

2 to 3 tablespoons wine vinegar

1. Pat the pieces dry with paper towels. Sprinkle them with salt and pepper.

2. In a large Dutch oven or other deep, heavy pot with a tight-fitting lid, heat the oil over medium heat. Add just enough lamb as will fit comfortably in one layer. Cook, stirring, to brown well on all sides. Transfer the browned meat to a plate. Continue with the remaining lamb.

3. When all the lamb has been browned, spoon off most of the fat from the pan. Add half the garlic, the sage, and the rosemary, and stir. Add the wine and cook 1 minute, scraping up and blending in the browned bits on the bottom of the pan with a wooden spoon.

4. Return the lamb pieces to the pan. Reduce the heat to low. Cover and cook, stirring occasionally, for 2 hours or until the lamb is tender and coming away from the bones. Add a little water if the liquid evaporates too rapidly.

5. To make the pesto: Chop the anchovies, rosemary, and remaining garlic together. Place them in a small bowl. Stir in just enough of the vinegar to form a paste.

6. Stir the pesto into the stew and simmer 5 minutes. Serve hot.

Lamb, Potato, and Tomato Stew

Stufato di Agnello e Verdure

Makes 4 to 6 servings

Though I usually use lamb shoulder for stew, I sometimes use trimmings left over from the leg or shank. The texture of these cuts is slightly chewier, but they require less cooking and still make a good stew. Notice that in this recipe from southern Italy, the meat is put into the pot all at once, so it is only lightly browned before the other ingredients are added.

1 large onion, chopped

2 tablespoons olive oil

2 pounds boneless leg or shank of lamb, cut into 1-inch chunks

Salt and freshly ground black pepper, to taste

½ cup dry white wine

3 cups drained and chopped canned tomatoes

1 tablespoon chopped fresh rosemary

1 pound waxy boiling potatoes, cut into 1-inch pieces

2 carrots, cut into ½-inch-thick slices

1 cup fresh peas or frozen peas, partially thawed

2 tablespoons chopped fresh flat-leaf parsley

1. In a large Dutch oven or other deep, heavy pot with a tight-fitting lid, cook the onion in the olive oil over medium heat until softened, about 5 minutes. Add the lamb. Cook, stirring frequently, until the pieces are lightly browned. Sprinkle with salt and pepper. Add the wine and bring it to a simmer.

2. Stir in the tomatoes and rosemary. Reduce the heat to low. Cover and cook 30 minutes.

3. Add the potatoes, carrots, and salt and pepper to taste. Simmer 30 minutes more, stirring occasionally, until the lamb and potatoes are tender. Add the peas and cook 10 minutes more. Sprinkle with parsley and serve immediately.

Lamb and Pepper Stew

Spezzato d'Agnello con Peperone

Makes 4 servings

The piquancy and sweetness of peppers and the richness of lamb make them two foods perfectly suited for each other. In this recipe, once the meat is browned, there is little to do except stir it occasionally.

¼ cup olive oil

2 pounds boneless lamb shoulder, cut into 1½-inch pieces

Salt and freshly ground black pepper, to taste

½ cup dry white wine

2 medium onions, sliced

1 large red bell pepper

1 large green bell pepper

6 plum tomatoes, peeled, seeded, and chopped

1. In a large casserole dish or Dutch oven, heat the oil over medium heat. Pat the lamb dry. Add just enough lamb to the pan as will fit comfortably in a single layer. Cook, stirring, until browned on all sides, about 20 minutes. Transfer the browned lamb to a plate. Continue cooking the remaining lamb in the same way. Sprinkle the meat all over with the salt and pepper.

2. When all the meat has been browned, spoon off excess fat. Add the wine to the pot and stir well, scraping up the browned bits. Bring to a simmer.

3. Return the lamb to the pot. Stir in the onions, peppers, and tomatoes. Reduce heat to low. Cover the pot and cook for $1^1/_2$ hours or until the meat is very tender. Serve hot.

Lamb Casserole with Eggs

Agnello Cacio e Uova

Makes 6 servings

Because eggs and lamb are both associated with springtime, it is only natural to pair them in recipes. In this dish, popular in one form or another throughout central and southern Italy, eggs and cheese form a light custardy topping on a lamb stew. It's a typical Easter recipe, so if you want to make it for the holiday meal, transfer the cooked stew to a pretty bake-and-serve casserole dish before adding the topping. A combination of lamb meat from the leg and shoulder makes for a more interesting texture.

2 tablespoons olive oil

2 medium onions

3 pounds boneless lamb leg and shoulder, trimmed and cut into 2-inch chunks

Salt and freshly ground black pepper to taste

1 tablespoon finely chopped rosemary

1½ cups homemade Meat Broth or Chicken Broth, or store-bought beef or chicken broth

2 cups shelled fresh peas or 1 (10-ounce) package frozen peas, partially thawed

3 large eggs

1 tablespoon chopped fresh flat-leaf parsley

½ cup freshly grated Pecorino Romano

1. Place a rack in the center of the oven. Preheat the oven to 425°F. In a Dutch oven or other deep, heavy pot with a tight-fitting lid, heat the oil over medium heat. Add the onion and lamb. Cook, stirring occasionally, until the lamb is lightly browned on all sides, about 20 minutes. Sprinkle with salt and pepper.

2. Add the rosemary and the broth. Stir well. Cover and bake, stirring occasionally, 60 minutes or until the meat is just tender. Add a little warm water if necessary to prevent the lamb from drying out. Stir in the peas and cook 5 minutes more.

3. In a medium bowl, beat the eggs, parsley, cheese, and salt and pepper to taste, until well blended. Pour the mixture evenly over the lamb.

4. Bake uncovered 5 minutes or until the eggs are just set. Serve immediately.

Lamb or Kid with Potatoes, Sicilian Style

Capretto o Agnello al Forno

Makes 4 to 6 servings

Baglio Elena, near Trapani in Sicily, is a working farm that produces olives, olive oil, and other foods. It is also an inn where visitors can stop for a meal in a charming, rustic dining room or stay for a vacation. When I visited, I was served a multicourse dinner of Sicilian specialties that included several types of olives prepared in different ways, excellent salame made on the premises, a variety of vegetables, and this simple stew. The meat and potatoes cook in no liquid other than a small amount of wine and the juices from the meat and vegetables, creating a symphony of flavors.

Kid is available in many ethnic butcher shops, including Haitian, Middle Eastern, and Italian. It is so similar to lamb that it can be hard to tell the difference.

3 pounds bone-in kid (young goat) or lamb shoulder, cut into 2-inch chunks

2 tablespoons olive oil

Salt and freshly ground black pepper

2 onions, thinly sliced

½ cup dry white wine

¼ teaspoon ground cloves

2 (2-inch) sprigs rosemary

1 bay leaf

4 medium all-purpose potatoes, cut into 1-inch pieces

2 cups cherry tomatoes, halved

2 tablespoons chopped fresh flat-leaf parsley

1. Place a rack in the center of the oven. Preheat the oven to 350°F. In a large Dutch oven or other deep, heavy pot with a tight-fitting lid, heat the oil over medium heat. Pat the lamb dry with paper towels. Add just enough meat to fit in the pot comfortably without crowding. Cook, turning the pieces with tongs until browned on all sides, about 15 minutes. Transfer the pieces to a plate. Continue cooking the remaining meat in the same way. Sprinkle with salt and pepper.

2. When all the meat has been browned, pour off most of the fat from the pan. Add the onion and cook, stirring occasionally, until the onion has wilted, about 5 minutes.

3. Return the meat to the pot. Add the wine and bring it to a simmer. Cook 1 minute, stirring with a wooden spoon. Add the cloves, rosemary, bay leaf, and salt and pepper to taste. Cover the pot and transfer it to the oven. Cook 45 minutes.

4. Stir in the potatoes and tomatoes. Cover and cook 45 minutes more or until the meat and potatoes are tender when pierced with a fork. Sprinkle with parsley and serve hot.

Apulian Lamb and Potato Casserole

Tiella di Agnello

Makes 6 servings

Layered casseroles baked in the oven are an Apulian specialty. They can be made with meat, fish, or vegetables, alternating with potatoes, rice, or bread crumbs. Tiella is a name given to both this method of cooking and the type of dish the casserole is cooked in. The classic tiella is a round deep dish made of terra cotta, though nowadays metal pans often are used.

The cooking method is most unusual. None of the ingredients is browned or precooked. Everything is simply layered and baked until tender. The meat will be well done, but still moist and delicious because the pieces are surrounded by the potatoes. The bottom layer of potatoes is meltingly soft and tender and full of the meat and tomato juices, while the top layer comes out as crisp as potato chips, though much more flavorful.

For the meat, use well-trimmed chunks of leg of lamb. I buy half of a butterflied leg of lamb at the supermarket, then I cut it at home into 2- to 3-inch chunks, trimming away the fat. It is just right for this recipe.

4 tablespoons olive oil

2 pounds baking potatoes, peeled and thinly sliced

½ cup plain dry bread crumbs

½ cup freshly grated Pecorino Romano or Parmigiano-Reggiano

1 garlic clove, finely chopped

½ cup chopped fresh flat-leaf parsley

1 tablespoon chopped fresh rosemary, or 1 teaspoon dried

½ teaspoon dried oregano

Salt and freshly ground black pepper

2½ pounds boneless lamb, trimmed and cut into 2- to 3-inch pieces

1 cup drained canned tomatoes, chopped

1 cup dry white wine

½ cup water

1. Place a rack in the center of the oven. Preheat the oven to 400°F. Spread 2 tablespoons of the oil in a 13 × 9 × 2–inch baking pan. Pat the potatoes dry and spread about half of them, overlapping slightly, on the bottom of the pan.

2. In a medium bowl, stir together the bread crumbs, cheese, garlic, herbs, and salt and pepper to taste. Scatter half of the crumb mixture over the potatoes. Arrange the meat on top of the crumbs. Season the meat with salt and pepper. Spread the tomatoes over the meat. Arrange the remaining potatoes on top. Pour in the wine and water. Scatter the remaining crumb mixture over all. Drizzle with the remaining 2 tablespoons olive oil.

3. Bake $1 1/2$ to $1 3/4$ hours or until the meat and potatoes are tender when pierced with a fork and everything is nicely browned. Serve hot.

Lamb Shanks with Chickpeas

Stinco di Agnello con Ceci

Makes 4 servings

Shanks need long, slow cooking, but when they are done, the meat is moist and just about melts in your mouth. If you purchase lamb shanks in the supermarket, the meat may need some extra trimming. With a small boning knife, cut away as much of the fat as possible, but leave intact the thin, pearly-looking covering on the meat known as the silver skin. It helps the meat to keep its shape as it cooks. I use shanks for a number of recipes that Italians would make with their smaller leg of lamb.

2 tablespoons olive oil

4 small lamb shanks, well trimmed

Salt and freshly ground black pepper

1 small onion, chopped

2 cups beef broth (Meat Broth)

1 cup peeled, seeded, and chopped tomatoes

½ teaspoon dried marjoram or thyme

4 carrots, peeled and cut into 1-inch pieces

2 tender celery ribs, cut into 1-inch chunks

3 cups cooked or 2 (16-ounce) cans chickpeas, drained

1. In a Dutch oven large enough to hold the shanks in a single layer, or another deep, heavy pot with a tight-fitting lid, heat the oil over medium heat. Pat the lamb shanks dry and brown them well on all sides, about 15 minutes. Tip the pan and spoon off the excess fat. Sprinkle with salt and pepper. Add the onion and cook 5 minutes more.

2. Add the broth, tomatoes, and marjoram and bring to a simmer. Reduce heat to low. Cover and cook 1 hour, turning the shanks occasionally.

3. Add the carrots, celery, and chickpeas. Cook 30 minutes more or until the meat is tender when pierced with a small knife. Serve hot.

Lamb Shanks with Peppers and Prosciutto

Brasato di Stinco di Agnello con Peperoni e Prosciutto

Makes 6 servings

In Senagalia, on the Adriatic coast in the Marches, I ate at the Osteria del Tempo Perso, in the historic center of this lovely old town. For a first course, I had cappelletti, stuffed "little hats" of fresh pasta with a sausage and vegetable sauce, followed by a lamb stew topped with bright-colored bell peppers and strips of prosciutto. I have adapted the flavors of the stew to lamb shanks in this recipe.

4 tablespoons olive oil

6 small lamb shanks, well trimmed

Salt and freshly ground black pepper

½ cup dry white wine

2-inch sprig fresh rosemary, or ½ teaspoon dried

1½ cups Meat Broth

2 red bell peppers, cut into ½-inch strips

1 yellow bell pepper, cut into ½-inch strips

1 tablespoon unsalted butter

2 ounces sliced imported Italian prosciutto, cut into thin strips

2 tablespoons chopped fresh flat-leaf parsley

1. In a Dutch oven just large enough to hold the lamb shanks in a single layer, or another deep, heavy pot with a tight-fitting lid, heat the oil over medium heat. Pat the lamb shanks dry. Brown them well on all sides, turning the pieces with tongs, about 15 minutes. Tip the pan and spoon off the excess fat. Sprinkle with salt and pepper.

2. Add the wine and cook, scraping up and blending in the browned bits at the bottom of the pan with a wooden spoon. Bring to a simmer and cook 1 minute.

3. Add the rosemary and broth and bring the liquid to a simmer.

4. Partially cover the pan. Reduce heat to low. Cook, turning the meat occasionally, until the lamb is very tender when pierced with a fork, about $1^{1}/_{4}$ to $1^{1}/_{2}$ hours.

5. While the lamb is cooking, in a medium saucepan, combine the peppers, butter, and 2 tablespoons of water over medium heat. Cover and cook 10 minutes, or until the vegetables are almost tender.

6. Add the softened peppers and the prosciutto to the lamb along with the parsley. Cook uncovered over medium heat until the peppers are tender, about 5 minutes.

7. With a slotted spoon, transfer the shanks and peppers to the warmed platter. Cover and keep warm. If the liquid left in the pan is too thin, raise the heat to high and boil until reduced and slightly thickened. Taste and adjust the seasoning. Pour the sauce over the lamb and serve immediately.

Lamb Shanks with Capers and Olives

Stinchi di Agnello con Capperi e Olive

Makes 4 servings

In Sardinia, goat meat is typically used for this dish. The flavors of lamb and goat are very similar, so lamb shanks are a good substitute and are a lot easier to find.

2 tablespoons olive oil

4 small lamb shanks, well trimmed

Salt and freshly ground black pepper

1 medium onion, chopped

¾ cup dry white wine

1 cup peeled, seeded, and chopped fresh or canned tomatoes

½ cup chopped pitted black olives, such as Gaeta

2 garlic cloves, finely chopped

2 tablespoons capers, rinsed and chopped

2 tablespoons chopped fresh flat-leaf parsley

1. In a Dutch oven large enough to hold the shanks in a single layer, or another deep, heavy pot with a tight-fitting lid, heat the oil over medium heat. Pat the lamb dry and brown it well on all sides. Spoon off the excess fat. Sprinkle with salt and pepper.

2. Scatter the onion around the lamb and cook until the onion is wilted, about 5 minutes. Add the wine and cook 1 minute. Stir in the tomatoes and bring to a simmer. Reduce the heat to low and cover the pan. Cook 1 to $1^1/_2$ hours, turning the shanks occasionally, until the meat is very tender when pierced with a knife.

3. Add the olives, garlic, capers, and parsley and cook 5 minutes more, turning the meat to coat with the sauce. Serve hot.

Lamb Shanks in Tomato Sauce

Stinco di Agnello al Pomodoro

Makes 6 servings

If the only lamb shanks you can find are on the large side, you can either have the butcher split them for you, or you can cook fewer shanks, leaving them whole, then carve the meat off the bone at serving time.

6 small lamb shanks, well trimmed

2 tablespoons olive oil

2 garlic cloves, thinly sliced

1 tablespoon chopped fresh rosemary

½ cup dry white wine

1 cup chopped peeled tomatoes

1½ cups beef broth (Meat Broth)

2 tablespoons chopped fresh flat-leaf parsley

1. In a Dutch oven large enough to hold the shanks in a single layer, or another deep, heavy pot with a tight-fitting lid, heat the oil. Brown the meat on all sides, about 15 minutes. Spoon off the excess fat. Sprinkle the shanks with salt and pepper.

2. Add the garlic and rosemary to the pan and cook 1 minute. Add the wine and bring to a simmer. Add the tomatoes and broth. Reduce the heat to low, cover the pan, and cook the shanks, turning them occasionally, about $1^1/_2$ hours or until the meat is fork tender and comes away easily from the bone.

3. Sprinkle with parsley and serve hot.

Lamb Pot Roast with Cloves, Roman Style

Garofolato di Agnello

Makes 6 servings

Cloves, called chiodi di garofalo in Italian, add a distinctive flavor to this lamb pot roast from the Roman countryside. The Romans use boned and rolled lamb shoulder, but if you can't find that cut, you can substitute leg of lamb with good results.

5 whole cloves

3½ pounds boneless lamb shoulder roast, rolled and tied

Salt and freshly ground black pepper

2 tablespoons olive oil

1 medium onion, finely chopped

1 tender celery rib, finely chopped

1 carrot, chopped

¼ cup chopped fresh flat-leaf parsley

A pinch of crushed red pepper

1 cup dry white wine

2 cups tomato puree

1 cup homemade Meat Broth or canned beef broth

1. Stick the cloves into the lamb. Sprinkle the meat all over with salt and pepper.

2. In a large casserole dish or Dutch oven, heat the oil over medium heat. Add the lamb and cook, turning it with tongs, until browned on all sides, about 20 minutes.

3. Scatter the onion, celery, carrot, parsley, and red pepper around the meat. Add the wine and cook until it evaporates, about 2 minutes. Add the tomato puree and broth. Reduce the heat to low.

4. Cover and cook, turning the meat occasionally, for $2^1/_2$ to 3 hours or until tender when pierced with a fork.

5. Transfer the meat to a cutting board. Cover and keep it warm. Skim the fat from the pan juices. Pour the vegetables and pan juices into a food processor or blender and puree until smooth. Taste and adjust seasoning. Pour the sauce into a medium saucepan and reheat it over low heat. If it is too thin, simmer it until reduced. Slice the lamb and serve hot with the sauce.

PASTRIES

Oranges in Orange Syrup

Arancia Marinate

Makes 8 servings

Juicy oranges in a sweet syrup are a perfect dessert after a rich meal. I especially like to serve these in winter when fresh oranges are at their best. Arranged on a platter, the oranges look very pretty with their topping of orange zest strips and glistening syrup. As a variation, cut the oranges into wedges and combine them with sliced ripe pineapple. Serve the orange sauce over all.

8 large navel oranges

1¼ cups sugar

2 tablespoons orange brandy or liqueur

1. Scrub the oranges with a brush. Trim off the ends. With a vegetable peeler, peel off the colored part of the orange skin (the zest) in wide strips. Avoid digging into the bitter white pith. Stack the zest strips and cut them into narrow matchstick pieces.

2. Remove the white pith from the oranges. Place the oranges on a serving platter.

3. Bring a small saucepan of water to a boil. Add the orange zest and bring to a simmer. Cook 1 minute. Drain the zest and rinse under cool water. Repeat. (This will help to remove some of the bitterness from the zest.)

4. Place the sugar and $1/4$ cup of water in another small saucepan over medium heat. Bring the mixture to a boil. Cook until the sugar is melted and the syrup thickens, about 3 minutes. Stir in the orange zest and cook 3 minutes more. Let cool.

5. Add the orange brandy to the contents of the pot. With a fork, remove the orange zest from the syrup and pile it on top of the oranges. Spoon on the syrup. Cover and chill up to 3 hours until ready to serve.

Oranges Gratinéed with Zabaglione

Arancia allo Zabaglione

Makes 4 servings

Gratiné is a French word meaning to brown the surface of a dish. Usually it applies to savory foods that are sprinkled with bread crumbs or cheese to help them brown.

Zabaglione is typically served plain or as a sauce for fruit or cake. Here it is spooned over oranges and broiled briefly until it browns slightly and forms a creamy topping. Bananas, kiwis, berries, or other soft fruits can also be prepared this way.

6 navel oranges, peeled and thinly sliced

Zabaglione

1 large egg

2 large egg yolks

⅓ cup sugar

⅓ cup dry or sweet Marsala

1. Preheat the broiler. Arrange the orange slices in a flameproof baking dish, overlapping slightly.

2. Prepare the zabaglione: Fill a small saucepan or the bottom of a double boiler with 2 inches of water. Bring it to a simmer over low heat. In a bowl larger than the rim of the pan or the top of the double boiler, combine the egg, yolks, sugar, and Marsala. Beat with a hand-held electric beater until foamy. Place over the pan of simmering water. Beat until the mixture is pale-colored and holds a soft shape when the beaters are lifted, about 5 minutes.

3. Spread the zabaglione over the oranges. Put the dish under the broiler 1 to 2 minutes or until the zabaglione is browned in spots. Serve immediately.

White Peaches in Asti Spumante

Pesche Bianche in Asti Spumante

Makes 4 servings

Asti Spumante is a sweet, sparkling dessert wine from Piedmont in northwestern Italy. It has a delicate orange-blossom flavor and aroma that comes from muscat grapes. If you can't find white peaches, yellow peaches will work well or substitute another summer fruit, such as nectarines, plums, or apricots.

4 large ripe white peaches

1 tablespoon sugar

8 ounces chilled Asti Spumante

1. Peel and pit the peaches. Cut them into thin slices.

2. Toss the peaches with the sugar and let stand 10 minutes.

3. Spoon the peaches into goblets or parfait glasses. Pour on the Asti Spumante and serve immediately.

Peaches in Red Wine

Pesche al Vino Rosso

Makes 4 servings

I remember watching my grandfather cutting up his homegrown white peaches to soak in a pitcher of red wine. The sweet peach juices tamed any roughness in the wine. White peaches are my favorite, but yellow peaches or nectarines are good too.

⅓ cup sugar, or to taste

2 cups fruity red wine

4 ripe peaches

1. In a medium bowl, combine the sugar and wine.

2. Cut the peaches in half and remove the pits. Cut the peaches into bite-size pieces. Stir them into the wine. Cover and refrigerate 2 to 3 hours.

3. Spoon the peaches and wine into goblets and serve.

Amaretti-Stuffed Peaches

Pesche al Forno

Makes 4 servings

This is a favorite dessert from Piedmont. Serve it drizzled with heavy cream or topped with a scoop of ice cream.

8 medium peaches, not too ripe

8 amaretti cookies

2 tablespoons softened unsalted butter

2 tablespoons sugar

1 large egg

1. Place a rack in the center of the oven. Preheat the oven to 375°F. Butter a baking dish large enough to hold the peach halves in a single layer.

2. Place the amaretti cookies in a plastic bag and crush them gently with a heavy object, such as a rolling pin. You should have about $1/2$ cup. In a medium bowl, mix together the butter and sugar and stir in the crumbs.

3. Following the line around the peaches, cut them in half and remove the pits. With a grapefruit spoon or a melon baller, scoop out a little of the peach flesh from the center to widen the opening and add it to the crumb mixture. Stir the egg into the mixture.

4. Arrange the peach halves cut sides up in the dish. Spoon some of the crumb mixture into each peach half.

5. Bake 1 hour or until the peaches are tender. Serve hot or at room temperature.

Pears in Orange Sauce

Pere all' Arancia

Makes 4 servings

When I visited Anna Tasca Lanza at Regaleali, her family's wine estate in Sicily, she gave me some of her excellent mandarin orange marmalade to take home. Anna uses the marmalade both as a spread and as a dessert sauce, and inspired me to stir some into the poaching liquid of some pears I was cooking. The pears had a beautiful golden glaze, and everyone loved the result. Now I make this dessert often. Because I quickly used up the supply of marmalade Anna gave me, I use quality store-bought orange marmalade.

½ cup sugar

1 cup dry white wine

4 firm ripe pears, such as Anjou, Bartlett, or Bosc

⅓ cup orange marmalade

2 tablespoons orange liqueur or rum

1. In a saucepan just large enough to hold the pears upright, combine the sugar and wine. Over medium heat, bring to a simmer and cook until the sugar is dissolved.

2. Add the pears. Cover the pan and cook about 30 minutes or until the pears are tender when pierced with a knife.

3. With a slotted spoon, transfer the pears to a serving platter. Add the marmalade to the liquid in the saucepan. Bring to a simmer and cook 1 minute. Remove from the heat and stir in the liqueur. Spoon the sauce over and around the pears. Cover and chill in the refrigerator at least 1 hour before serving.

Pears with Marsala and Cream

Pere al Marsala

Makes 4 servings

I had pears prepared this way at a trattoria in Bologna. If you prepare them just before eating dinner, they will be at the right serving temperature when you are ready for dessert.

You can find both dry and sweet Marsala imported from Sicily, though the dry is of better quality. Either can be used for making desserts.

4 large Anjou, Bartlett, or Bosc pears, not too ripe

¼ cup sugar

½ cup water

½ cup dry or sweet Marsala

¼ cup heavy cream

1. Peel the pears and cut them in half lengthwise.

2. In a skillet large enough to hold the pear halves in a single layer, bring the sugar and water to a simmer over medium heat. Stir to

dissolve the sugar. Add the pears and cover the skillet. Cook 5 to 10 minutes or until the pears are almost tender when pierced with a fork.

3. With a slotted spoon, transfer the pears to a plate. Add the Marsala to the skillet and bring to a simmer. Cook until the syrup is slightly thickened, about 5 minutes. Stir in the cream and simmer 2 minutes more.

4. Return the pears to the skillet and baste them with the sauce. Transfer the pears to serving dishes and spoon the sauce over the top. Let cool to room temperature before serving.

Pears with Warm Chocolate Sauce

Pere Affogato al Cioccolato

Makes 6 servings

Sweet fresh pears bathed in a bittersweet chocolate sauce is a classic European dessert. I had this in Bologna, where the chocolate sauce was made with Majani chocolate, a locally made brand that unfortunately does not travel far from its hometown. Use a good-quality bittersweet chocolate. One brand that I like, Scharffen Berger, is made in California.

6 Anjou, Bartlett, or Bosc pears, not too ripe

2 cups water

¾ cup sugar

4 (2 × ½–inch) strips orange zest, cut into matchsticks

1½ cups Warm Chocolate Sauce

1. Peel the pears, leaving the stems intact. With a melon baller or small spoon, scoop out the core and seeds, working from the bottom of the pears.

2. In a saucepan large enough to hold all the pears upright, bring the water, sugar, and orange zest to a simmer over medium heat. Stir until the sugar is dissolved.

3. Add the pears and reduce the heat to low. Cover the pan and cook, turning the pears once, for 20 minutes or until tender when pierced with a small knife. Let the pears cool in the syrup.

4. When ready to serve, prepare the chocolate sauce.

5. With a slotted spoon, transfer the pears to serving dishes. (Cover and refrigerate the syrup for another use, such as tossing with cut-up fruits for a salad.) Drizzle with warm chocolate sauce. Serve immediately.

Rum-Spiced Pears

Pere al Rhum

Makes 6 servings

The sweet, mild, almost floral taste of ripe pears lends itself to many other complementary flavors. Fruits such as oranges, lemons, and berries and many cheeses go well with them, and Marsala and dry wines are often used to poach pears. In Piedmont I was pleasantly surprised to be served these pears simmered in a spiced rum syrup accompanying a simple hazelnut cake.

6 Anjou, Bartlett, or Bosc pears, not too ripe

¼ cup brown sugar

¼ cup dark rum

¼ cup water

4 whole cloves

1. Peel the pears, leaving the stems intact. With a melon baller or small spoon, scoop out the core and seeds, working from the bottom of the pears.

2. In a saucepan just large enough to hold the pears, stir together the sugar, rum, and water over medium heat until the sugar is melted, about 5 minutes. Add the pears. Scatter the cloves around the fruit.

3. Cover the pan and bring the liquid to a simmer. Cook over medium-low heat 15 to 20 minutes or until the pears are tender when pierced with a knife. With a slotted spoon, transfer the pears to a serving dish.

4. Simmer the liquid uncovered until reduced and syrupy. Strain the liquid over the pears. Let cool.

5. Serve at room temperature or cover and chill in the refrigerator.

Spiced Pears with Pecorino

Pere allo Spezie e Pecorino

Makes 6 servings

Tuscans are rightly proud of their excellent sheep's milk cheese. Every town has its own version, and each tastes slightly different from the others, depending on how it is aged and where the milk comes from. Usually the cheeses are eaten when they are quite young and still semifirm. When eaten for dessert, the cheese is sometimes drizzled with a little honey or served with pears. I like this sophisticated presentation that I had in Montalcino—pecorino served with pears cooked in the local red wine and spices, accompanied by fresh walnuts.

Of course, the pears are also good served plain or with a large spoonful of whipped cream.

6 medium Anjou, Bartlett, or Bosc pears, not too ripe

1 cup dry red wine

½ cup sugar

1 (3-inch) piece cinnamon stick

4 whole cloves

8 ounces Pecorino Toscano, Asiago, or Parmigiano-Reggiano cheese, cut into 6 pieces

12 walnut halves, toasted

1. Place a rack in the center of the oven. Preheat the oven to 450°F. Arrange the pears in a baking dish just large enough to hold them upright.

2. Stir together the wine and sugar until the sugar softens. Pour the mixture over the pears. Scatter the cinnamon and cloves around the pears.

3. Bake the pears, basting them occasionally with the wine, 45 to 60 minutes or until they are tender when pierced with a knife. If the liquid begins to dry up before the pears are done, add a little warm water to the pan.

4. Let the pears cool in the dish, basting them occasionally with the pan juices. (As the juices cool, they thicken and coat the pears with a rich red glaze.) Remove the spices.

5. Serve the pears with the syrup at room temperature or slightly chilled. Place them on serving dishes with two walnut halves and a piece of the cheese.

Roasted Brussels Sprouts

Cavolini al Forno

Makes 4 to 6 servings

If you have never tried roasted brussels sprouts, you will be amazed at how good they taste. I roast them until they are nice and brown. The outer leaves get crisp while the insides remain soft. These are great with roast pork.

1 pound brussels sprouts

⅓ cup olive oil

Salt

3 garlic cloves, sliced

1. With a small knife, shave a thin slice off the base of the brussels sprouts. Cut them in half through the base.

2. Preheat the oven to 375°F. Pour the oil into a roasting pan large enough to hold the sprouts in a single layer. Add the sprouts, salt, and garlic. Toss well and turn the sprouts cut-side down.

3. Roast the sprouts, stirring once, 30 to 40 minutes, or until browned and tender. Serve hot.

Brussels Sprouts with Pancetta

Cavolini di Bruxelles al Pancetta

Makes 4 to 6 servings

Garlic and pancetta flavor these sprouts. Substitute bacon for the pancetta for a hint of smoky flavor.

1 pound brussels sprouts

Salt to taste

2 tablespoons olive oil

2 thick slices of pancetta (2 ounces), cut into matchstick strips

4 large garlic cloves, thinly sliced

Pinch of crushed red pepper

1. With a small knife, shave a thin slice off the base of the brussels sprouts.

2. Bring a large pot of water to a boil. Add the sprouts and salt to taste. Cook until the sprouts are almost tender, about 5 minutes.

3. In a large skillet, cook the pancetta in the oil until lightly golden, about 5 minutes. Add the garlic and crushed red pepper and cook until the garlic is golden, about 2 minutes more.

4. Add the brussels sprouts, 2 tablespoons of water, and a sprinkle of salt. Cook, stirring occasionally, until the sprouts are tender and beginning to brown, about 5 minutes. Serve hot.

Browned Cabbage with Garlic

Cavolo al'Aglio

Makes 4 servings

Cabbage cooked this way tastes nothing like the bland and soggy vegetable we all love to hate. I always thought that overcooking ruined cabbage, but in this case, like the roasted brussels sprouts above, long, slow cooking browns the cabbage and gives it a rich, sweet flavor. I first tasted it at Manducatis, a restaurant in Long Island City whose owners come from Montecassino in Italy.

1 medium head of cabbage (about 1½ pounds)

3 large garlic cloves, finely chopped

Crushed red pepper

¼ cup olive oil

Salt

1. Trim off the outer leaves of the cabbage. With a large heavy chef's knife, cut the cabbage into quarters. Cut out the core. Cut the cabbage into bite-size pieces.

2. In a large pot, cook the garlic and red pepper in the olive oil over medium-low heat until the garlic is golden, about 2 minutes.

3. Add the cabbage and salt. Stir well. Cover and cook, stirring often, for 20 minutes, or until the cabbage is lightly browned and tender. Add a little water if the cabbage begins to stick. Serve hot.

Shredded Cabbage with Capers and Olives

Cavolo al Capperi

Makes 4 servings

Olives and capers dress up shredded cabbage. If you don't want to buy a whole cabbage, try making this using a bag of undressed coleslaw from the produce section of the supermarket. The brand I buy is a combination of white cabbage, a little red cabbage, and carrots. It works perfectly in this recipe.

4 tablespoons olive oil

1 small head of cabbage (about 1 pound)

About 3 tablespoons water

1 to 2 tablespoons white wine vinegar

Salt

½ cup chopped green olives

1 tablespoon chopped capers

1. Trim off the outer leaves of the cabbage. With a large heavy chef's knife, cut the cabbage into quarters. Cut out the core. Cut the quarters crosswise into narrow strips.

2. In a large pot, heat the oil over medium heat. Add the cabbage, water, vinegar, and a small amount of salt. Stir well.

3. Cover the pot and turn the heat to low. Cook until the cabbage is almost tender, about 15 minutes.

4. Stir in the olives and capers. Cook until the cabbage is very tender, about 5 minutes more. If there is a lot of liquid left in the pan, uncover and cook until it evaporates. Serve hot.

Cabbage with Smoked Pancetta

Verze con Pancetta Affumicata

Makes 6 servings

Here is another traditional Friulian recipe inspired by chef Gianni Cosetti. Gianni uses smoked pancetta for this recipe, but you can substitute bacon or smoked ham.

2 tablespoons olive oil

1 medium onion, chopped

2 ounces chopped smoked pancetta, bacon, or ham

½ medium head of cabbage, thinly sliced

Salt and freshly ground black pepper

1. In a large pot, cook the oil, onion, and pancetta for 10 minutes or until golden.

2. Stir in the cabbage and salt and pepper to taste. Lower the heat. Cover and cook 30 minutes or until very soft. Serve hot.

Fried Cardoons

Cardoni Fritti

Makes 6 servings

Here is a basic recipe for cardoons: they are boiled, coated with bread crumbs, and fried until crisp. These are good as part of an antipasto assortment or as a side dish with lamb or fish.

1 lemon, cut in half

2 pounds cardoons

3 large eggs

2 tablespoons freshly grated Parmigiano-Reggiano

Salt and freshly ground black pepper

2 cups plain bread crumbs

Vegetable oil for frying

Lemon wedges

1. Squeeze the lemon into a large bowl of cold water. Trim the ends of the cardoons and separate the stalk into ribs. With a paring knife, peel each rib to remove the long tough strings and any leaves. Cut each rib into 3-inch lengths. Place the pieces in the lemon water.

2. Bring a large saucepan of water to a boil. Drain the cardoons and add them to the pan. Boil until tender when pierced with a knife, about 20 to 30 minutes. Drain well and cool under running water. Pat the pieces dry.

3. Line a tray with paper towels. In a shallow bowl, beat the eggs with the cheese, salt, and pepper to taste. Spread the bread crumbs on a sheet of wax paper. Dip the cardoons in the egg, then roll them in the bread crumbs.

4. In a large deep skillet, heat about $1/2$ inch of oil over medium heat until a small drop of the egg sizzles and cooks rapidly when dropped into the pan. Add just enough of the cardoons to fit in one layer without crowding. Cook, turning the pieces with tongs, until browned and crisp on all sides, about 3 to 4 minutes. Drain on the paper towels. Keep them warm in a low oven while frying the remainder. Serve hot with lemon wedges.

Cardoons with Parmigiano-Reggiano

Cardoni alla Parmigiana

Makes 6 servings

Cardoons taste delicious baked with butter and Parmigiano.

1 lemon, cut in half

About 2 pounds cardoons

Salt and freshly ground pepper

3 tablespoons unsalted butter

½ cup freshly grated Parmigiano-Reggiano

1. Prepare the cardoons as in Fried Cardoons through step 2.

2. Place a rack in the center of the oven. Preheat the oven to 450°F. Generously butter a 13 × 9 × 2– inch baking pan.

3. Arrange the cardoon pieces in the pan. Dot with the butter and sprinkle with salt and pepper. Scatter the cheese over the top.

4. Bake 10 to 15 minutes, or until the cheese is slightly melted. Serve hot.

Cardoons in Cream

Cardoni alla Panna

Makes 6 servings

These cardoons are simmered in a skillet with a little cream. Parmigiano-Reggiano provides the finishing touch.

1 lemon, cut in half

About 2 pounds cardoons

2 tablespoons unsalted butter

Salt and freshly ground black pepper

½ cup heavy cream

½ cup freshly grated Parmigiano-Reggiano

1. Prepare the cardoons as in Fried Cardoons through step 2.

2. In a large skillet, melt the butter over medium heat. Add the cardoons and salt and pepper to taste. Stir until coated with the butter, about 1 minute.

3. Add the cream and bring to a simmer. Cook until the cream is slightly thickened, about 1 minute. Sprinkle with cheese and serve hot.

Carrots and Turnips with Marsala

Misto di Rape e Carote

Makes 4 servings

Sweet, nutty-tasting Marsala enhances the flavor of root vegetables like carrots and turnips.

4 medium carrots

2 medium turnips, or 1 large rutabaga

2 tablespoons unsalted butter

Salt

¼ cup dry Marsala

1 tablespoon chopped fresh flat-leaf parsley

1. Peel the carrots and turnips and cut them into 1-inch pieces.

2. In a large skillet, melt the butter over medium heat. Add the vegetables and salt to taste. Cook for 5 minutes, stirring occasionally.

3. Add the Marsala. Cover and cook 5 minutes more or until the wine evaporates and the vegetables are tender. Sprinkle with parsley and serve immediately.

Roasted Carrots with Garlic and Olives

Carote al Forno

Makes 4 servings

Carrots, garlic, and olives are a surprisingly good combination, with the saltiness of the olives playing off the sweetness of the carrots. I had these in Liguria, near the border with France.

8 medium carrots, peeled and cut diagonally into 1/2-inch-thick slices

2 tablespoons olive oil

3 garlic cloves, sliced

Salt and freshly ground black pepper

1/2 cup pitted imported mild black olives, such as Gaeta

1. Place a rack in the center of the oven. Preheat the oven to 425°F. In a large baking pan, toss the carrots with the oil, garlic, and salt and pepper to taste.

2. Roast 15 minutes. Stir in the olives and cook until the carrots are tender, about 5 minutes more, Serve hot.

Carrots in Cream

Carote alla Panna

Makes 4 servings

Carrots are so often eaten raw, we forget how good they can be when cooked. In this recipe, heavy cream complements their sweet flavor.

8 medium carrots

2 tablespoons unsalted butter

Salt

½ cup heavy cream

Pinch of grated nutmeg

1. Peel the carrots. Cut them into $1/4$-inch thick slices.

2. In a medium saucepan over medium heat, melt the butter. Add the carrots and salt to taste. Cover and cook, stirring occasionally, until the carrots are softened, about 5 minutes.

3. Stir in the cream and nutmeg. Cook until the cream is thickened and the carrots are tender, 4 to 5 minutes more. Serve immediately.

Sweet-and-Sour Carrots

Carote in Agrodolce

Makes 4 servings

I like to serve these carrots with roast pork or chicken. If you have some parsley, mint, or basil on hand, chop the herb and toss it with the carrots just before serving.

8 medium carrots

1 tablespoon unsalted butter

3 tablespoons white wine vinegar

2 tablespoons sugar

Salt

1. Peel the carrots. Cut them into $1/4$-inch-thick slices.

2. In a medium saucepan, melt the butter over medium heat. Add the vinegar and sugar and stir until the sugar is dissolved. Stir in the carrots and salt to taste. Cover the pot and cook until the carrots are softened, about 5 minutes.

3. Uncover the pan and cook the carrots, stirring frequently, until tender, about 5 minutes more. Taste for seasoning. Serve hot or at room temperature.

Marinated Eggplant with Garlic and Mint

Melanzane Marinate

Makes 4 to 6 servings

This is excellent as a side dish with grilled chicken or as part of an antipasto assortment. Zucchini and carrots can also be prepared this way.

2 medium eggplants (about 1 pound each)

Salt

Olive oil

3 tablespoons red wine vinegar

2 garlic cloves, finely chopped

¼ cup chopped fresh mint

Freshly ground black pepper

1. Trim the tops and bottoms of the eggplants. Cut the eggplants crosswise into ½-inch-thick slices. Arrange the slices in a colander, sprinkling each layer with salt. Place the eggplant over

a plate to drain for at least 30 minutes. Rinse off the salt with cool water and dry the slices with paper towels.

2. Preheat the oven to 450°F. Brush the eggplant slices with the oil and arrange them oiled-side down in a single layer on cookie sheets. Brush the tops with oil. Bake the slices for 10 minutes. Turn and bake until browned and tender, about 10 minutes more.

3. In a shallow plastic container with a tight-fitting lid, make a layer of the eggplant slices, overlapping them slightly. Sprinkle with vinegar, garlic, mint, and pepper. Repeat the layering until all of the ingredients are used.

4. Cover and refrigerate for at least 24 hours before serving. These keep well for several days.

Grilled Eggplant with Fresh Tomato Salsa

Melanzane alla Griglia con Salsa

Makes 4 servings

Here, eggplant slices are grilled, then topped with a fresh tomato salsa. Serve with burgers, steaks, or chops. I had eggplant prepared this way in Abruzzo, where fresh green chiles are often used. Substitute crushed red pepper from a jar if you prefer.

1 medium eggplant (about 1 pound)

Salt

3 tablespoons olive oil

1 medium ripe tomato

2 tablespoons chopped fresh flat-leaf parsley

1 tablespoon finely chopped fresh chile (or to taste)

1 teaspoon fresh lemon juice

1. Trim the tops and bottoms of the eggplants. Cut the eggplant crosswise into $1/2$-inch-thick slices. Arrange the slices in a colander, sprinkling each layer with salt. Place the eggplant over

a plate to drain for at least 30 minutes. Rinse off the salt with cool water and dry the slices with paper towels.

2. Place a barbecue grill or broiler rack about 5 inches away from the heat source. Preheat the grill or broiler Brush the eggplant slices with olive oil on one side and place them with the oiled side toward the source of the heat. Cook until lightly browned, about 5 minutes. Turn the slices and brush them with oil. Cook until browned and tender, about 4 minutes.

3. Arrange the slices on a platter, overlapping slightly.

4. Cut the tomato in half and squeeze out the seeds and juice. Chop the tomato. In a medium bowl, toss the tomato with the parsley, chile, lemon juice, and salt to taste. Spoon the tomato mixture over the eggplant. Serve at room temperature.

Eggplant and Mozzarella "Sandwiches"

Panini di Mozzarella

Makes 6 servings

I sometimes add a folded slice of prosciutto to these "sandwiches" and serve them as an antipasto. Spoon on a little tomato sauce if you have some, and sprinkle with grated Parmigiano if you like.

2 medium eggplants (about 1 pound each)

Salt

Olive oil

Freshly ground black pepper

1 tablespoon chopped fresh thyme or flat-leaf parsley

8 ounces fresh mozzarella, thinly sliced

1. Trim the tops and bottoms of the eggplants. With a swivel-blade peeler, remove strips of skin lengthwise at about 1-inch intervals. Cut the eggplants crosswise into an even number of $1/2$-inch thick slices. Arrange the slices in a colander, sprinkling each layer with salt. Place the colander over a plate to drain for at least 30 minutes. Rinse off the salt with cool water and dry the slices with paper towels.

2. Preheat the oven to 450°F. Brush the eggplant slices with olive oil and arrange them oiled-side down in a single layer on cookie sheets. Brush the tops with additional oil. Sprinkle with pepper and the herbs. Bake 10 minutes. Turn the slices and bake about 10 minutes more, or until lightly browned and tender.

3. Remove the the eggplants from the oven, but leave the oven turned on.

4. Top half of the eggplant slices with mozzarella. Place the remaining eggplant slices on top. Return the pans to the oven for 1 minute or until the cheese begins to melt. Serve hot.

Eggplant with Garlic and Herbs

Melanzane al Forno

Makes 6 to 8 servings

I like to use long, slim Japanese eggplants when I see them at my farmer's market during the summer months. They are very good for summer meals simply roasted with garlic and herbs.

3 tablespoons olive oil

8 small Japanese eggplants (all about the same size)

1 garlic clove, very finely chopped

2 tablespoons chopped fresh basil

Salt and freshly ground black pepper

1. Place a rack in the center of the oven. Preheat the oven to 400°F. Oil a large baking pan.

2. Trim the stem ends from the eggplants and cut them in half lengthwise. Cut several shallow slits in the cut surfaces. Arrange the eggplants cut-sides up in the baking pan.

3. In a small bowl, mix together the oil, garlic, basil, and salt and pepper to taste. Spread the mixture over the eggplants, pushing a little into the slits.

4. Bake 25 to 30 minutes or until the eggplants are tender. Serve hot or at room temperature.

Neapolitan-Style Eggplant Sticks with Tomatoes

Bastoncini di Melanzane

Makes 4 servings

At Restaurant Dante and Beatrice in Naples, meals begin with a series of small appetizers. Sticks of small eggplants in a fresh tomato and basil sauce are one of the dishes my husband and I enjoyed there. Japanese eggplants are milder than the large globe variety, but either kind can be used for this recipe.

6 small Japanese eggplants (about 1½ pounds)

Vegetable oil for frying

Salt

2 garlic cloves, peeled and lightly smashed

Pinch of crushed red pepper

3 tablespoons olive oil

4 plum tomatoes, peeled, seeded, and chopped

¼ cup basil leaves, stacked and cut into thin strips

1. Trim the tops and bottoms of the eggplants and cut them into 6 wedges lengthwise. Cut crosswise into 3 pieces. Pat the pieces dry with paper towels.

2. Line a tray with paper towels. Pour about $1/2$ inch of the oil into a medium skillet. Heat over medium heat until a small piece of eggplant sizzles when added to the pan. Carefully add just as many eggplants as will fit comfortably in the pan in a single layer. Cook, stirring occasionally, until lightly browned around the edges, about 5 minutes. Remove the eggplants with a slotted spoon or skimmer and drain on the paper towels. Repeat with the remaining eggplant. Sprinkle with salt.

3. In a large skillet, cook the garlic with the red pepper in the olive oil until the garlic is deep golden, about 4 minutes. Remove and discard the garlic. Add the tomatoes and cook 5 minutes or until thickened.

4. Stir in the eggplants and basil and cook 2 minutes more. Season with salt to taste. Serve hot or at room temperature

Eggplant Stuffed with Prosciutto and Cheese

Melanzane Ripiene

Makes 6 servings

Cousins and uncles and aunts came from all over the region the first time my husband Charles and I went to visit his relatives, who live near the famous Valley of the Temples in Agrigento in Sicily. Each family unit wanted us to visit their home, have a meal, and stay overnight. We wanted to spend time with everyone, but we also wanted to see some of the local historical sites that we had always heard so much about, and we only had a few days. Fortunately, my husband's cousin Angela took charge and made sure that we were well taken care of. When I told her I was interested in the local cooking, she taught me how to make this delicious eggplant dish.

6 small eggplants (about 1½ pounds)

Salt

¼ cup olive oil

1 medium onion, chopped

1 medium tomato

2 eggs, beaten

½ cup grated caciocavallo, provolone, or Parmigiano-Reggiano

¼ cup finely chopped fresh basil

2 ounces imported Italian prosciutto, finely chopped

½ cup plus 1 tablespoon unflavored bread crumbs

Salt and freshly ground black pepper

1. Trim off the tops of the eggplants and cut them in half lengthwise. With a small sharp knife and a spoon, scoop out the pulp of the eggplants, leaving the shells about ¼ inch thick. Chop the eggplant pulp.

2. Place the chopped eggplant in a colander. Sprinkle generously with salt and let drain over a plate at least 30 minutes. Sprinkle the eggplant shells with salt and place them cut-sides down on a plate to drain.

3. Rinse off the salt with cool water and dry the eggplant with paper towels. Squeeze the pulp to extract the water.

4. In a medium skillet, heat the oil over medium heat. Add the onion and chopped eggplant and cook, stirring frequently, until tender, about 15 minutes. Scrape the mixture into a bowl.

5. Cut the tomato in half and squeeze out the seeds and juice. Chop the tomato and add it to the bowl. Stir in the eggs, cheese, basil, prosciutto, 1/2 cup bread crumbs, and salt and pepper to taste. Mix well.

6. Place a rack in the center of the oven. Preheat the oven to 400°F. Oil a baking pan just large enough to hold the eggplant shells in a single layer.

7. Fill the shells with the eggplant mixture, rounding the surface. Place them in the pan. Sprinkle with the 1 tablespoon bread crumbs. Pour 1/4 cup of water around the eggplants. Bake 45 to 50 minutes or until the shells are tender when pierced. Serve hot or at room temperature.

Eggplant Stuffed with Anchovies, Capers, and Olives

Melanzane Ripiene

Makes 4 servings

There seems to be no limit to the Sicilian ways to cook eggplant. This one combines the classic flavors of anchovies, olives, and capers.

2 medium eggplants (about 1 pound each)

Salt

¼ cup plus 1 tablespoon olive oil

1 large garlic clove, finely chopped

2 medium tomatoes, peeled, seeded, and chopped

6 anchovy fillets

½ cup chopped Gaeta or other mild black olives

2 tablespoons capers, rinsed and drained

½ teaspoon dried oregano

⅓ cup plain dry bread crumbs

1. Trim off the tops of the eggplants. Cut the eggplants in half lengthwise. With a small sharp knife and a spoon, scoop out the eggplant pulp, leaving a shell about ½ inch thick. Coarsely chop the pulp and place it in a colander. Sprinkle generously with salt and set over a plate to drain. Sprinkle the insides of the eggplant shells with salt and place them upside down on paper towels. Let drain for 30 minutes.

2. Rinse off the salt with cool water and dry the eggplant with paper towels. Squeeze the pulp to extract the water.

3. Heat the oil in a large skillet over medium-high heat until a small piece of eggplant sizzles when added to the pan. Add the eggplant pulp and cook, stirring frequently, until it begins to brown, 15 to 20 minutes. Stir in the garlic and cook 1 minute. Add the tomatoes, anchovies, olives, capers, oregano, and salt and pepper to taste. Cook until thickened, about 5 minutes more.

4. Place a rack in the center of the oven. Preheat the oven to 400°F. Oil a baking pan just large enough to hold the eggplant shells in a single layer.

5. Fill the shells with the eggplant mixture. Place them in the pan. Toss the bread crumbs with the remaining oil and sprinkle them

over the shells. Bake 45 minutes or until the shells are tender when pierced. Let cool slightly. Serve warm or at room temperature.

Eggplant with Vinegar and Herbs

Melanzane alle Erbe

Makes 6 to 8 servings

Plan to make this at least an hour before serving. Letting it sit will give the vinegar a chance to mellow. I like to serve this with grilled tuna or swordfish as part of a summer barbecue.

2 medium eggplants (about 1 pound each) cut into 1-inch pieces

Salt

½ cup olive oil

½ cup red wine vinegar

¼ cup sugar

2 tablespoons chopped fresh flat-leaf parsley

2 tablespoons chopped fresh mint

1. Trim the tops and bottoms of the eggplants. Cut the eggplants into 1-inch pieces. Place the pieces in a colander, sprinkling each layer with salt. Place the colander over a plate to drain for at

least 30 minutes. Rinse off the salt with cool water and pat the pieces dry with paper towels.

2. Line a tray with paper towels. Heat $1/4$ cup of the oil in a large skillet over medium heat. Add half the eggplant pieces and cook, stirring frequently, until browned, about 15 minutes. With a slotted spoon, transfer the eggplant to the paper towels to drain. Add the remaining oil to the skillet and fry the remaining eggplant in the same way.

3. Remove the skillet from the heat and carefully pour off any remaining oil. Carefully wipe out the skillet with paper towels.

4. Place the skillet over medium heat and add the vinegar and sugar. Stir until the sugar is dissolved. Return all of the eggplant to the skillet and cook, stirring, until the liquid is absorbed, about 5 minutes.

5. Transfer the eggplant to a serving dish and sprinkle with the parsley and mint. Let cool. Serve at room temperature.

Fried Eggplant Cutlets

Melanzane Fritte

Makes 4 to 6 servings

The only difficulty with these cutlets is that it's hard to stop eating them. They are so good when hot and freshly made. Serve them in sandwiches or as a side dish.

1 medium eggplant (about 1 pound)

Salt

2 large eggs

¼ cup freshly grated Parmigiano-Reggiano

Freshly ground black pepper

½ cup all-purpose flour

1½ cups plain dry bread crumbs

Vegetable oil for frying

1. Trim the tops and bottoms of the eggplants. Cut the eggplant crosswise into ¼-inch-thick slices. Arrange the slices in a

colander, sprinkling each layer with salt. Place the colander over a plate to drain for at least 30 minutes. Rinse off the salt with cool water and dry the slices with paper towels.

2. Put the flour in a shallow bowl. In another shallow bowl, beat together the eggs, cheese, and salt and pepper to taste. Dip the eggplant slices into the flour, then in the egg mixture, then in the bread crumbs, patting to coat well. Let the slices dry on a rack for 15 minutes.

3. Line a tray with paper towels. Turn the oven on to the lowest setting. In a large heavy skillet, heat $1/2$ inch of oil until a small drop of the egg mixture sizzles when it touches the oil. Add just enough of the eggplant slices to fit in a single layer without crowding. Fry until golden brown on one side, about 3 minutes, then turn them over and brown on the other side, about 2 to 3 minutes more. Drain the eggplant slices on the paper towels. Keep them warm in a low oven while frying the remainder in the same way. Serve hot.

Eggplant with Spicy Tomato Sauce

Melanzane in Salsa

Makes 6 to 8 servings

This layered dish is similar to eggplant parmigiana—without the Parmigiano. Because there is no cheese, it is lighter and fresher—nice for summer meals.

2 medium eggplants (about 1 pound each)

Salt

Olive oil

2 garlic cloves, crushed

2 cups tomato puree

$\frac{1}{2}$ teaspoon crushed red pepper

$\frac{1}{2}$ cup torn fresh basil leaves

1. Trim the tops and bottoms of the eggplants. Cut the eggplants crosswise into $1/2$-inch-thick slices. Arrange the slices in a colander, sprinkling each layer with salt. Place the colander over

a plate to drain for at least 30 minutes. Rinse off the salt with cool water and dry the slices with paper towels.

2. Place a rack in the center of the oven. Preheat the oven to 450°F. Brush two large jelly roll pans with oil. Arrange the eggplant slices in a single layer. Brush with oil. Bake until lightly browned, about 10 minutes. Turn the slices with a metal spatula and bake until the second side is browned and the slices are tender when pierced, about 10 minutes more.

3. In a medium saucepan, cook the garlic in $1/4$ cup olive oil over medium heat until golden, about 2 minutes. Add the tomato puree, red pepper, and salt to taste. Simmer for 15 minutes or until thick. Discard the garlic.

4. In a shallow dish, arrange half the eggplant in a single layer. Spread with half the sauce and basil. Repeat with the remaining ingredients. Serve at room temperature.

Eggplant Parmigiana

Melanzane alla Parmigiana

Makes 6 to 8 servings

This is one of those dishes I never tire of. If you prefer not to fry the eggplant, try making this with grilled or baked slices.

2½ cups Marinara Sauce or other plain tomato sauce

2 medium eggplants (about 1 pound each)

Salt

Olive oil or vegetable oil for frying

8 ounces fresh mozzarella, sliced

½ cup freshly grated Parmigiano-Reggiano or Pecorino Romano

1. Prepare the sauce, if necessary. Then, trim the tops and bottoms off the eggplants. Cut the eggplants crosswise into ¹/₂-inch-thick slices. Arrange the slices in a colander, sprinkling each layer with salt. Place the colander over a plate to drain for at least 30 minutes. Rinse off the salt with cool water and dry the slices with paper towels.

2. Line a tray with paper towels. Heat about $1/2$ inch of the oil in a large skillet over medium heat until a small piece of eggplant sizzles when added to the pan. Add just enough of the eggplant slices to fit in a single layer without crowding. Fry until golden brown on one side, about 3 minutes, then turn them over and brown on the other side, about 2 to 3 minutes more. Drain the slices on the paper towels. Cook the remaining eggplant slices in the same way.

3. Place a rack in the center of the oven. Preheat the oven to 350°F. Spread a thin layer of tomato sauce in a 13 × 9 × 2–inch baking dish. Make a layer of eggplant slices, overlapping them slightly. Top with a layer of mozzarella, another layer of sauce, and a sprinkle of grated cheese. Repeat the layering, ending with eggplant, sauce, and grated cheese.

4. Bake for 45 minutes, or until the sauce is bubbling. Let stand 10 minutes before serving.

Roasted Fennel

Finocchio al Forno

Makes 4 servings

When I was growing up, we never ate fennel cooked. It was always served raw, adding a refreshing crunchiness to salads or served in wedges after a meal, especially big holiday feasts. But baking tames some of the flavor and changes the texture, so that it becomes soft and tender.

2 medium fennel bulbs (about 1 pound)

¼ cup olive oil

Salt

1. Place a rack in the center of the oven. Preheat the oven to 425°F. Trim off the green stalks of the fennel down to the rounded bulb. Pare away any bruises with a small knife or vegetable peeler. Slice off a thin layer from the root end. Cut the fennel in half lengthwise. Cut each half lengthwise into $1/2$-inch-thick slices.

2. Pour the oil into a 13 × 9 × 2–inch baking pan. Add the fennel slices and turn them to coat with oil. Arrange the slices in a single layer. Sprinkle with salt.

3. Cover the pan with foil. Bake 20 minutes. Uncover and bake 15 to 20 minutes more or until the fennel is tender when pierced with a knife. Serve hot or at room temperature.

Fennel with Parmesan Cheese

Finocchio alla Parmigiano

Makes 6 servings

This fennel is simmered in water first to make it extra tender. Then it is topped with grated Parmigiano and baked. Serve this with roast veal or pork.

2 small fennel bulbs (about 1 pound)

Salt

2 tablespoons unsalted butter

Freshly ground black pepper

¼ cup grated Parmigiano-Reggiano

1. Place a rack in the center of the oven. Preheat the oven to 450°F. Generously butter a 13 × 9 × 2– inch baking dish.

2. Trim off the green stalks of the fennel down to the rounded bulb. Parc away any bruises with a small knife or vegetable peeler. Slice off a thin layer from the root end. Cut the bulbs lengthwise through the core into ¼-inch-thick slices.

3. In a large pot, bring 2 quarts of water to a boil. Add the fennel and 1 teaspoon salt. Reduce the heat and simmer uncovered, until the fennel is crisp-tender, 8 to 10 minutes. Drain well and pat dry.

4. Arrange the fennel slices in a single layer in the baking dish. Dot with the butter and sprinkle with salt and pepper to taste. Top with the cheese. Bake 10 minutes, or until the cheese is lightly browned. Serve hot or at room temperature.

Fennel with Anchovy Sauce

Finocchio con Salsa di Acciughe

Makes 4 servings

Instead of tenderizing the fennel by boiling it, in this recipe you cover and bake it, allowing it to steam in its own juices. The flavor remains intact, and the fennel turns out slightly crunchy yet still tender. If you prefer fennel softer, boil it as in the recipe for Fennel with Parmesan Cheese.

Because fennel cooked this way is so tasty, I like to serve it with unadorned grilled chicken or pork chops. This also makes a good antipasto dish at room temperature.

2 medium fennel bulbs (about one pound)

4 anchovy fillets, drained and chopped

2 tablespoons chopped fresh flat-leaf parsley

2 tablespoons capers, rinsed and drained

Freshly ground black pepper

Salt (optional)

¼ cup olive oil

1. Place a rack in the center of the oven. Preheat the oven to 375°F. Oil a 13 × 9 × 2–inch baking dish.

2. Trim off the green stalks of the fennel down to the rounded bulb. Pare away any bruises with a small knife or vegetable peeler. Slice off a thin layer from the root end. Cut the bulbs lengthwise through the core into ¼-inch-thick slices.

3. Arrange the fennel in a single layer in the pan, overlapping the slices slightly. Scatter the anchovies, parsley, capers, and pepper over the top. Add salt, if desired. Drizzle with the oil.

4. Cover the pan with aluminum foil. Bake 40 minutes or until the fennel is tender. Carefully remove the foil and bake 5 minutes more, or until the fennel is just tender when pierced, but not soft. Let cool slightly before serving.

Green Beans with Parsley and Garlic

Fagiolini al Aglio

Makes 4 servings

Fresh parsley is essential in the Italian kitchen. I always keep a bunch in my refrigerator. When I bring it home from the store, I trim the ends and stick the stems in a jar of water. Covered with a plastic bag, parsley stays fresh at least a week in the refrigerator, especially if I am careful about changing the water in the jar. Wash parsley before using it to eliminate any grit, and pinch the leaves off the stems. Chop the parsley on a board with a large chef's knife, or if you prefer, just tear it into bits. Fresh chopped parsley adds color and freshness to many foods.

As a variation, give these beans a final toss in the skillet with some grated lemon zest before serving.

1 pound green beans

Salt

3 tablespoons olive oil

1 garlic clove, finely chopped

2 tablespoons chopped fresh flat-leaf parsley

Freshly ground black pepper

1. Snap off the stem ends of the green beans. Bring about 2 quarts of water to a boil in a large saucepan. Add the beans and salt to taste. Cook uncovered until the beans are crisp-tender, 4 to 5 minutes.

2. Drain the beans and pat them dry. (If you are not using them immediately, cool them under cold running water. Wrap the beans in a kitchen towel and leave at room temperature up to 3 hours.)

3. Just before serving, heat the oil with the garlic and parsley in a large pan over medium heat. Add the beans and a sprinkle of pepper. Toss gently 2 minutes until just hot. Serve hot.

Green Beans with Hazelnuts

Fagiolini al Nocciole

Makes 4 servings

Walnuts and almonds are good with these beans too, if you prefer.

1 pound green beans

Salt

3 tablespoons unsalted butter

1/3 cup chopped hazelnuts

1. Snap off the stem ends of the green beans. Bring about 2 quarts of water to a boil in a large saucepan. Add the beans and salt to taste. Cook uncovered until the beans are crisp-tender, 4 to 5 minutes.

2. Drain the beans well and pat them dry. (If you are not using them immediately, cool them under cold running water. Wrap the beans in a kitchen towel and leave at room temperature up to 3 hours.)

3. Just before serving, heat the butter in a large pan. Add the hazelnuts and cook, stirring often, until the nuts are lightly toasted and the butter is lightly browned, about 3 minutes.

4. Add the beans and a pinch of salt. Cook, stirring often, until heated, 2 to 3 minutes. Serve immediately.

Green Beans with Green Sauce

Fagiolini al Pesto

Makes 4 servings

Add some boiled new potatoes to these green beans, if you like. Serve them with grilled salmon steaks or tuna.

    1/4 cup Green Sauce

1 pound green beans

Salt

1. Prepare the green sauce, if necessary. Then, snap off the stem ends of the green beans. Bring about 2 quarts of water to a boil in a large saucepan. Add the beans and salt to taste. Cook uncovered until the beans are tender, 5 to 6 minutes.

2. Drain the beans well and pat them dry. Toss with the sauce. Serve warm or at room temperature.

Green Bean Salad

Fagiolini in Insalata

Makes 6 servings

Anchovies and fresh herbs add zest to this green bean salad. If you like, add some strips of roasted red bell peppers.

1½ pounds green beans

4 anchovy fillets

2 garlic cloves, finely chopped

2 tablespoons chopped fresh flat-leaf parsley

1 tablespoon chopped fresh mint

¼ cup olive oil

2 tablespoons red wine vinegar

Salt and freshly ground black pepper

1. Snap off the stem ends of the green beans. Bring about 2 quarts of water to a boil in a large saucepan. Add the beans and salt to taste. Cook uncovered until the beans are tender, 5 to 6 minutes.

2. Rinse the beans under cold water and drain well. Pat dry.

3. In a medium bowl, combine the anchovies, garlic, parsley, mint, and salt and pepper to taste. Whisk in the oil and vinegar.

4. Toss the green beans with the dressing and serve.

Green Beans in Tomato-Basil Sauce

Fagiolini in Salsa di Pomodoro

Makes 6 servings

These go well with grilled sausages or ribs.

1½ pounds green beans

Salt

2 tablespoons unsalted butter

1 small onion, finely chopped

2 cups peeled, seeded, and chopped fresh tomatoes

Freshly ground black pepper

6 fresh basil leaves, torn into bits

1. Snap off the stem ends of the green beans. Bring about 2 quarts of water to a boil in a large saucepan. Add the beans and salt to taste. Cook uncovered until the beans are crisp-tender, 4 to 5 minutes. Rinse the beans under cold water and drain well. Pat dry.

2. In a medium saucepan, melt the butter over medium heat. Add the onion and cook, stirring frequently, until golden, about 10 minutes. Add the tomatoes and salt and pepper to taste. Bring to a simmer and cook 10 minutes.

3. Stir in the green beans and basil. Cook until heated through, about 5 minutes more.

Green Beans with Pancetta and Onion

Fagiolini alla Pancetta

Makes 6 servings

Green beans are more flavorful and have a better texture when cooked until tender. Exact cooking time depends on the size, freshness, and maturity of the beans. I usually taste one or two to be sure. I like them when they no longer snap but are not soft or mushy. This recipe is from Friuli–Venezia Giulia.

1 pound green beans

Salt

½ cup chopped pancetta (about 2 ounces)

1 small onion, chopped

2 garlic cloves, finely chopped

2 tablespoons chopped fresh flat-leaf parsley

2 fresh sage leaves

2 tablespoons olive oil

1. Snap off the stem ends of the green beans. Bring about 2 quarts of water to a boil in a large saucepan. Add the beans and salt to taste. Cook uncovered until the beans are crisp-tender, 4 to 5 minutes. Rinse the beans under cold water and drain well. Pat dry. Cut the beans into bite-size pieces.

2. In a large skillet, cook the pancetta, onion, garlic, parsley, and sage in the oil over medium heat until the onion is golden, about 10 minutes. Add the green beans and a pinch of salt. Cook until heated through, about 5 minutes more. Serve hot.

Green Beans with Tomato and Pancetta Sauce

Fagiolini con Salsa di Pomodori e Pancetta

Makes 4 servings

These beans make a great meal with a frittata or omelet.

1 pound green beans

Salt

¼ cup chopped pancetta (about 1 ounce)

1 garlic clove, finely chopped

2 tablespoons olive oil

2 large ripe tomatoes, peeled, seeded, and chopped

2 sprigs fresh rosemary

Freshly ground black pepper

1. Prepare the beans as described in step 1 of the Green Beans with Pancetta and Onion recipe, but do not cut them into pieces.

2. In a medium saucepan, cook the pancetta and garlic in the oil over medium heat until golden, about 5 minutes. Stir in the

tomatoes, rosemary, and salt and pepper to taste. Bring to a simmer and cook 10 minutes.

3. Stir the beans into the sauce and cook until heated through, about 5 minutes. Remove the rosemary. Serve hot.

Green Beans with Parmigiano

Fagiolini alla Parmigiana

Makes 4 servings

Lemon zest, nutmeg, and cheese flavor these green beans. Use fresh ingredients for best results.

1 pound green beans, trimmed

2 tablespoons butter

1 small onion, chopped

½ teaspoon grated fresh lemon zest

Pinch of freshly ground nutmeg

Salt and freshly ground black pepper

¼ cup freshly grated Parmigiano-Reggiano

1. Snap off the stem ends of the green beans. Bring about 2 quarts of water to a boil in a large saucepan. Add the beans and salt to taste. Cook uncovered until the beans are crisp-tender, 4 to 5 minutes. Rinse the beans under cold water and drain well. Pat dry.

2. In a medium skillet, melt the butter over medium heat. Add the onion and cook until golden, about 10 minutes. Stir in the beans, lemon zest, nutmeg, and salt and pepper to taste. Sprinkle with the cheese and remove from the heat. Let the cheese melt a little and serve hot.

Wax Beans with Olives

Fagiolini Giallo con Olive

Makes 4 servings

Shiny black olives and green parsley offer a vibrant color contrast for pale yellow wax beans; green beans taste good prepared this way, too. To serve these beans at room temperature, substitute olive oil for the butter, which would firm up as it cooled.

1 pound yellow wax or green beans

Salt

3 tablespoons unsalted butter

1 small onion, chopped

1 garlic clove, finely chopped

½ cup mild black olives, such as Gaeta, pitted and chopped

2 tablespoons chopped fresh flat-leaf parsley

1. Snap off the stem ends of the green beans. Bring about 2 quarts of water to a boil in a large saucepan. Add the beans and salt to taste. Cook uncovered until the beans are crisp-tender, 4 to 5

minutes. Rinse the beans under cold water and drain well. Pat dry. Cut the beans into 1-inch pieces.

2. In a skillet large enough to hold all of the beans, melt the butter over medium heat. Add the onion and garlic and cook until tender and golden, about 10 minutes.

3. Stir in the beans, olives, and parsley until heated through, about 2 minutes. Serve hot.

Spinach with Lemon

Spinaci al Limone

Makes 4 servings

A drizzle of good olive oil and a few drops of fresh lemon juice perk up the flavor of cooked spinach or other leafy greens.

2 pounds fresh spinach, tough stems removed

¼ cup water

Salt

Extra-virgin olive oil

Lemon wedges

1. Wash the spinach well in several changes of cold water. Put the spinach, water, and a pinch of salt in a large pot. Cover the pot and turn on the heat to medium. Cook 5 minutes or until the spinach is wilted and tender. Drain the spinach and press out the excess water.

2. In a serving bowl, toss the spinach with olive oil to taste.

3. Serve, hot or at room temperature, garnished with lemon wedges.

Spinach or Other Greens with Butter and Garlic

Verdura al Burro

Makes 6 servings

The mellowness of butter and garlic goes particularly well with the slight bitterness of greens such as spinach or Swiss chard.

2 pounds spinach, tough stems removed

¼ cup water

Salt

2 tablespoons unsalted butter

1 garlic clove, finely chopped

Freshly ground black pepper

1. Wash the spinach well in several changes of cold water. Put the spinach, water, and a pinch of salt in a large pot. Cover the pot and turn on the heat to medium. Cook 5 minutes or until the spinach is wilted and tender. Drain the spinach and press out the excess water.

2. In a medium skillet, melt the butter over medium heat. Add the garlic and cook until golden, about 2 minutes.

3. Stir in the spinach and salt and pepper to taste. Cook, stirring occasionally, until heated through, about 2 minutes. Serve hot.

Spinach with Raisins and Pine Nuts

Spinaci con Uva e Pinoli

Makes 4 servings

Raisins and pine nuts are used to flavor many dishes in southern Italy and throughout the Mediterranean. Swiss chard or beet greens can also be prepared this way.

2 pounds fresh spinach, tough stems removed

¼ cup water

Salt

2 tablespoons unsalted butter

Freshly ground black pepper

2 tablespoons raisins

2 tablespoons pine nuts, toasted

1. Wash the spinach well in several changes of cold water. Put the spinach, water, and a pinch of salt in a large pot. Cover the pot and turn on the heat to medium. Cook 5 minutes or until the

spinach is wilted and tender. Drain the spinach and press out the excess water.

2. Wipe out the pot. Melt the butter in the pot, then add the spinach and raisins. Stir once or twice and cook 5 minutes until the raisins are plump. Sprinkle with the pine nuts and serve immediately.

Spinach with Anchovies, Piedmont Style

Spinaci alla Piemontesa

Makes 6 servings

In Piedmont, this savory spinach is often served on slices of bread fried in butter, but it is also good on its own. Another variation is to top the spinach with fried or poached eggs.

2 pounds fresh spinach, tough stems removed

¼ cup water

Salt

¼ cup unsalted butter

4 anchovy fillets

1 garlic clove, finely chopped

1. Wash the spinach well in several changes of cold water. Put the spinach, water, and a pinch of salt in a large pot. Cover the pot and turn on the heat to medium. Cook 5 minutes or until the spinach is wilted and tender. Drain the spinach and press out the excess water.

2. Wipe out the pot. Melt the butter in the pot. Add the anchovies and garlic and cook, stirring, until the anchovies dissolve, about 2 minutes. Stir in the spinach and cook, stirring constantly, until heated through, 2 to 3 minutes. Serve hot.

Escarole with Garlic

Scarola al'Aglio

Makes 4 servings

Escarole is a member of the large and varied chicory family, which includes endive, frisée, dandelion, and radicchio. Escarole is very popular in Neapolitan kitchens. Small heads of escarole are stuffed and braised, tender inner leaves are eaten raw in salads, and escarole is also cooked in soup. Vary this dish by leaving out the red pepper and adding ¼ cup of raisins.

1 head escarole (about 1 pound)

3 tablespoons olive oil

3 garlic cloves, thinly sliced

Pinch of crushed red pepper (optional)

Salt

1. Trim the escarole and discard any bruised leaves. Cut off the stem ends. Separate the leaves and wash well in cool water, especially in the center of the leaves where soil collects. Stack the leaves and cut them into bite-size pieces.

2. In a large pot, cook the garlic and red pepper, if using, in the olive oil over medium heat until the garlic is golden, about 2 minutes. Add the escarole and salt to taste. Stir well. Cover the pot and cook until the escarole is tender, about 12 to 15 minutes. Serve hot.

Dandelion with Potatoes

Dente di Leone con Patate

Makes 4 servings

Kale or chard can be substituted for the dandelion greens—you need a vegetable firm enough to cook at the same time as the potatoes. A bit of wine vinegar sparks up the flavor of these garlicky greens and potatoes.

1 bunch dandelion greens (about 1 pound)

6 small waxy potatoes, peeled and sliced

Salt

3 garlic cloves, chopped

3 tablespoons olive oil

1 tablespoon white wine vinegar

1. Trim the dandelion and discard any bruised leaves. Cut off the stem ends. Separate the leaves and wash well in cool water, especially in the center of the leaves where soil collects. Cut the leaves crosswise into bite-size pieces.

2. Bring about 4 quarts of water to a boil. Add the potato slices, dandelion, and salt to taste. Bring the water back to the boil and cook until the vegetables are tender, about 10 minutes. Drain well.

3. In a large skillet, cook the garlic in the oil until golden, about 2 minutes. Add the vegetables, vinegar, and a pinch of salt. Cook, stirring well, until heated through, about 2 minutes. Serve hot.

Mushrooms with Garlic and Parsley

Funghi Trifolati

Makes 4 servings

This is probably the most popular way to prepare mushrooms in Italy. Try adding some exotic mushroom varieties for more flavor.

1 (10- to 12-ounce) package white mushrooms

¼ cup olive oil

2 tablespoons chopped fresh flat-leaf parsley

2 large garlic cloves, thinly sliced

Salt and freshly ground black pepper

1. Place the mushrooms in a colander and rinse them quickly under cold running water. Drain the mushrooms and pat them dry. Cut the mushrooms into halves or quarters if large. Trim off the ends if they look dry.

2. In a large skillet, heat the oil over medium heat. Add the mushrooms. Cook, stirring often, until the mushrooms are browned, 8 to 10 minutes. Add the parsley, garlic, salt, and pepper. Cook until the garlic is golden, about 2 minutes more. Serve hot.

Mushrooms, Genoa Style

Funghi alle Erbe

Makes 6 servings

The hillsides around Genoa are full of wild mushrooms and herbs, so naturally cooks there use them in many ways. Porcini mushrooms are typically used for this dish, though any large cultivated mushroom can be substituted. Because porcini are not often available in the United States, I substitute meaty and flavorful portobello mushrooms. I sometimes serve them as the centerpiece for a meatless meal.

6 large portobello mushrooms

4 tablespoons olive oil

Salt and freshly ground black pepper

2 garlic cloves, finely chopped

3 tablespoons finely chopped fresh flat-leaf parsley

1 teaspoon chopped fresh rosemary

½ teaspoon dried marjoram

1. Place a rack in the center of the oven. Preheat the oven to 425°F. Oil a baking pan large enough to hold the mushroom caps in a single layer.

2. Wipe the mushrooms clean with damp paper towels. Snap off the stems of the mushrooms and trim the ends where soil collects. Thinly slice the stems. Place the mushroom stems in a bowl and toss them with 2 tablespoons of the oil.

3. Place the mushroom caps open-side up in the pan. Sprinkle with salt and pepper.

4. In a small bowl, stir together the garlic, parsley, rosemary, marjoram, and salt and pepper to taste. Toss with the remaining 2 tablespoons oil. Place a pinch of the herb mixture on each mushroom cap. Top with the stems.

5. Bake 15 minutes. Check the mushrooms to see if the pan is too dry. Add a little warm water if needed. Bake 15 minutes more or until tender. Serve hot or at room temperature.

Roasted Mushrooms

Funghi al Forno

Makes 4 to 6 servings

In the spring and fall, when they are most plentiful, porcini mushrooms are roasted in olive oil until lightly browned around the edges yet tender and meaty inside. Porcini are rare and expensive in the United States, but you can apply the same treatment to other thick, fleshy mushroom varieties, such as cremini, portobello, or white mushrooms, with good results. Don't crowd the pan, though, as some varieties give off a lot of water and the mushrooms will steam instead of turning brown.

1 pound mushrooms, such as white, cremini, or portobello

4 large garlic cloves, thinly sliced

¼ cup extra-virgin olive oil

Salt and freshly ground black pepper

1. Place a rack in the center of the oven. Preheat the oven to 400°F. Wipe the mushrooms clean with damp paper towels. Snap off the stems of the mushrooms and trim the ends where soil collects. Cut the mushrooms into quarters, or eighths if large. In

a roasting pan large enough to hold the ingredients in a single layer, toss the mushrooms, garlic, and oil with salt and pepper to taste. Spread them evenly in the pan.

2. Roast 30 minutes, stirring once or twice, until the mushrooms are tender and browned. Serve hot.

www.ingramcontent.com/pod-product-compliance
Lightning Source LLC
Chambersburg PA
CBHW071817080526
44589CB00012B/829